LOVEBIRDS
A QUARTERLY

This is a comprehensive text for practicing bird fanciers. It is designed as a useful guide for the ever more numerous lovebird fanciers. It is my wish and also my hope that this book wins even more friends for the lovebirds, as well as helps them to select their first birds and to resolve any minor problems.

It is hoped that those who have known these charming short-tailed little parrots for some time already will also find much useful information in the many pages of this book.

Unlike an introductory survey or identification guide, this practical book contains a lot of accumulated experience on the birds described herein, and I would like to pass on as much of my experience as possible.

I have not included the Black-Collared lovebird *Agapornis swinderniana*, whose German name is translated as *green-head*, and ask you to understand that I didn't want to sacrifice any space for theoretical bird descriptions; I've never yet seen a living specimen and perhaps neither have you.

All lovebirds are natural members of a small, closely related African parrot family, so mixed breeding of the individual specimens held in bird fanciers' aviaries and cages quickly occurs, especially in the progeny of smaller holdings, thus producing birds which are no longer pure.

The eight main species covered in this practical guide have been divided, as is common practice now, into those *with* white eye rings (periorbital rings) and those *without* them. Other noteworthy differences in appearance, nest building habits, etc., will be presented in very detailed and comprehensive descriptions of the individual species. I think most readers will agree with me that a complete cataloging of all regions of Africa where the lovebirds are distributed will not be of very much use to the fancier. Nor will I report on their behavior in the wild, for astonishingly little is known about it, despite the fact that lovebirds themselves have been known for quite some time.

Many fanciers of these small, colorful parrot-billed Africans firmly believe that they are moving up to second place among the aviculturists and that their color varieties still have a great future ahead of them. In any case, lovebirds are charming pets that any bird fancier can keep, care for and also breed—which is true even for beginners, at least with two or three species.

I'm convinced that the great popularity of lovebirds will grow even more, as will the number of exciting color varieties, such as we have for the budgerigar.

These cute bird couples with their bright, glossy plumage are quite unpretentious, easy to feed, affordable, take little space and can be bred successfully—so many advantages do not often show up together in other parrots!

Agapornis, from the Greek words for *love* and *birds*, gave us the English name of the species—*lovebird*. The German name is similar but slightly more functional, and is translated as "the inseparables."

Even if you haven't had any previous experience, I'm rather certain that you'll soon come to love these comical little imps, and perhaps I just may contribute a bit to your love for lovebirds.

Karl-Herbert Delpy

Karl-Herbert Delpy is one of Germany's most knowledgeable breeders and writers of lovebirds. This book, originally published in Germany where it became an instant best-seller, was written for a German audience, but the information is so fascinating, that the American publisher, T.F.H., is bringing it to you enhanced with 75 additional color illustrations!

ABOUT QUARTERLIES

T.F.H. quarterlies are published in both magazine format and normal book format, at different prices of course. The concept behind this type of publishing is getting the information to you as quickly and reasonably priced as possible. Magazine formats are accustomed to being produced in 30 days; books have almost no time limit. Thus our **Quarterlies** are published by our magazine staff.

yearBOOKS,INC.
Dr. Herbert R. Axelrod,
Founder & Chairman
Neal Pronek
Chief Editor
Linda A. Lindner
Editor

yearBOOKS are all photo composed, color separated and designed on Scitex equipment in Neptune, N.J. with the following staff:

DIGITAL PRE-PRESS
Michael L. Secord
Supervisor
Bernie Gaglia
Robert Onyrscuk
Computer Art
Sherise Buhagiar
Patti Escabi
Cynthia Fleureton
Sandra Taylor Gale
Pat Marotta
Joanne Muzyka

Advertising Sales
George Campbell
Chief
Amy Manning
Director
Jennifer Feidt
Coordinator

©yearBOOKS,Inc.
1 TFH Plaza
Neptune, N.J. 07753
Completely manufactured in Neptune, N.J.
USA

CONTENTS

INTRODUCTION

For almost three decades now I've continued to feel all the unaltered fascination and wonderment I felt very early onE in my long career as a fancier of lovebirds. These handy and manageable little Africans belong to the most beautiful, charming, agile, and yet most unpretentious representatives of the great, many-membered parrot family. And I love them quite specially.

The German name "inseparables," which is also preferred by the French, is solidly entrenched among bird hobbyists. We shouldn't call the lovebirds dwarf parrots or parrotlets (*Forpus* spp) or hanging parrots (*Loriculus* spp), nor squeeze them all together into one pigeonhole just because of certain similarities in size or behavior.

Our little Africans, the lovebirds, are gregarious, thick-headed, short-tailed, small parrots. Because of their small size, their craving for movement is not such a problem for the hobbyist, who often worries about the limited amount of available space.

The intensity of lovebird calls, especially in small flocks, could possibly swell to such a level that close neighbors might complain. As a precaution, I should also mention a certain aggressiveness towards other birds in the same enclosure.

Lovebirds captured in the wild are not often imported into any country in large numbers. On the other hand, the most popular ones have already been bred for decades in all of Europe, so a rather reasonably priced supply of many species is always available.

For groups or for breeding, the preferred way to keep lovebirds is undoubtedly in aviary or flight enclosures under a roof, or in an actual garden aviary built up against a shelter. There are enough reports on successful longterm

Photo by Dr. Herbert R. Axelrod.

A magnificent Masked Lovebird, *Agapornis personata*. This species is not the most popular of all lovebirds and yet it exists in many color varieties.

housing, care and breeding in large cages too.

Bird fanciers' tastes vary, and not every parrot fan also becomes a lovebird admirer. What I am offering here is a somewhat small book that still contains a great deal of material and provides a complete picture of the lovebirds, including some general knowledge, practical tips and good advice for the lovebird fancier.

THE DAYS OF EXPLORERS

It's been at least two centuries now since lovebirds were first described in detail. Astonishingly, the first species were ones only rarely kept today, namely *Agapornis cana* and *Agapornis pullaria* (known since 1603!).

Several Madagascar or Gray-headed Lovebirds ended up at the London Zoo in the mid-19th century, *Agapornis swinderniana* and *Agapornis taranta* were discovered and described. This was reported in the book *Shelby's Parrots,* published in 1836. Even today the older books refer to *Agapornis selby.*

Agapornis taranta appears to have been first introduced much later than its discovery, namely in 1906 in Vienna. The "little red-fronted parrot" *(Agapornis roseicollis)* must have been known for quite some time in Austria. The natural history collection of Ferdinand I of Austria contains a splendid painting by the court painter Leopold Brunner, who depicts two lovebirds facing each other on a branch. Here's a contemporary account from those days, now preserved in the Austrian National Library: "They are called the inseparables because they can only be kept in couples, otherwise they will die quickly of loneliness. They are small parrots of predominantly green color, from South Africa and Madagascar. Almost all the world's parrot species lead an exemplary monogamous married life. The lovebirds, however, carry even fidelity beyond the grave. They don't speak, but do maintain a touching moral ideal which is also a model for humankind. How charmingly the painter Brunner has them facing one another, as if communing, and has understood how to portray them for all eternity." And that's homage in the idiom of that time to the lovebirds described in this book.

In another bird book over a hundred years old, I once read that the first *Agapornis* species discovered was *Agapornis roseicollis*, that is, it was already discovered by the end of the 18th century. Reports are not always as reliable as one would have them.

A few years after World War I, and after inflation subsided, the established lovebird fanciers were overjoyed with the introduction of Black-masked and Fischer's specimens (1925-1926). The triggering event was Dr. G.A. Fischer's expedition to Lake Victoria. *Agapornis lilianae* was discovered in 1927. We have an Englishman, Dr. Kirkmann, to thank for discovering the Black-cheeked Lovebird, which he first saw in 1904 and described in 1906 in a publication of the Ornithologists Club in 1920.

Agapornis swinderniana was discovered in the Congo valley in present-day Gabon. Reichnow and Neumann also claim having described two subspecies for the first time; the actual discoverers, however, were probably G. Zenker and Emin Pascha. Only a few of the Black-collared Lovebirds *(A. swinderniana)* have been seen in Europe up to now, and some scant published information on it is supposed to be found in Belgium, which was a colonial power in the Congo.

Someone once told me that good reports on African bird lore are also found among church-related book collections, to which ornithologically inclined missionaries have contributed their writings. It must be fascinating to track down

Peach-faced Lovebirds have been bred for hundreds of generations in aviaries and cages of bird lovers all over the world. Attractive color variations are often inbred to produce new varieties. This photo shows a normal and abnormally colored Peach-face.

Photo by Dr. Herbert R. Axelrod

something like that, but where do you start searching?

The largest number of lovebird imports into Germany was by Carl Hagenbeck, of Hamburg, in some cases dating back a hundred years. Today, the number of bird importers has increased, although they are predominantly smaller businesses. For many of the birds described in this work, the source countries in Africa have instituted export restrictions.

It might be possible that the species not included in this book—the Black-collared Lovebird *(Agapornis swinderniana)*, which has been protected up to now, may one day be able to reach us in great numbers, thus representing to a certain extent a new discovery for fanciers of the genus *Agapornis.*

Lovebird breeder Bischoff mounted and led an expedition a few years ago for the sole purpose of observing this allegedly not rare bird at least once alive in the wild. He was unsuccessful.

There is apparently not much to support any great hopes of finding one, especially considering the difficulty of capturing a living bird which lives on river banks in thick rainforest.

The possibility of yet more, still unknown lovebird species in Africa is one of the hypotheses which are becoming more and more improbable. Breeders have the best chances of coming up with new, or at least novel-looking, color varieties.

One of the earliest portraits of the Peach-faced Lovebird was this lovely drawing by Eric Peake.

FEEDING, DRINKING, BATHING

Feeding lovebirds is hardly more difficult than feeding budgerigars. Under some circumstances, it can be important that feeding not be completely dependent upon commercially available foods. Thank goodness that what parrots eat is partly a matter of habit! The individual lovebird descriptions also contain some information on food preferences or recommendations.

All lovebirds are so-called granivores. Don't take that too literally, as if the bird were not interested in anything else, for that would be wrong, of course. Grains or seeds are the *main* food, the most important of which are: sunflower seeds (small-kernel varieties, white, black, and striped); millet (also in sprays); hemp seed; canary seed; oats (hulled and unhulled); light millet varieties; Japanese millet; Niger seed; grass seed; weed seed.

Quite individualistic tastes have often been observed in lovebirds. Here's an important rule: what a bird gobbles up first, preferentially and in large amounts is not necessarily healthy or very digestible! Feed components (particularly hemp, Niger and oats) that metabolize easily into fatty deposits may have to be rationed, at least sometimes. Sunflower seeds don't really belong to the feed components which need to rationed, particularly because the birds like so much to eat them. Now, however, seeds grown for their higher fat content predominate, which is good for oil manufacturers, but not so good for our ornamental birds. But you can resolve that by selecting only the colorful, small-kernel varieties.

Parrots need fixed proportions of such things as

Photo by Dr. Herbert R. Axelrod

An early color variety was this lutino Peach-faced Lovebird. This is essentially an abnormal color produced when the black (melanophores) pigment is missing in the feathers.

proteins, carbohydrates, fats, minerals, vitamins and trace elements, as well as roughage, all of which in their own way affect health and well-being. The scope of this book doesn't allow me to go into more detail on that.

For adult birds there is no single natural food that contains all the foregoing components in sufficient quantities—which is why a broadly varied mixture is recommended. You can freely substitute one to three seeds from time to time.

Small packages of feed are available for birds. Try out the feed and check on the percentage of feed utilization. Perhaps the birds have to get used to it. Packaged or prepared feed relieves you somewhat of the burden, and perhaps also risky storage. It also guarantees the greatest possible cleanliness as well as year' round consistency of quality and composition. Bird feed is bought in larger quantities only by those who have proper (dry and ventilated) storage facilities available. Overstocked, dust-ridden and mite-infested feedstuff, or feeds contaminated with the excreta of vermin, are a danger, so wholesale prices are not always worth the risk.

Proper nutrition is always an essential element in caring for ornamental birds, and it is especially true for feeding during the breeding season, as proper nutrition plays a critical role in successful breeding.

In other periods of stress, too, such as when the birds molt or stay outside in the garden aviary in winter, increased amounts of fat- and oil-rich seeds are useful and can be given. Logically, of course, oil-rich seeds are not advisable during hot weather.

Packaged budgerigar feed can be given to all lovebirds for variety from time to time, such as during emergencies when you run out of the usual lovebird feed. You can readily see that the experienced fancier doesn't keep his lovebirds on the same diet day after day, all year long. If, for whatever reason, you have to feed your birds monotonously, or have only limited possibilities of obtaining a greater variety, the birds won't be suddenly exposed to any danger because of it; but they'll probably just forego some minor advantage apparent only to the experts.

While our lovebirds are still young is when they most easily adapt to eating unfamiliar or infrequently eaten foods. The older parrots get, the more reserved and suspicious they become towards the unknown. New food items which are still disliked frequently can be mixed in with especially liked seeds and given in the morning when the birds are particularly hungry.

The question of whether parent birds with especially efficient food-utilization metabolisms can transmit that characteristic to their offspring seems dubious to me, although some authors recommend preferential breeding with such birds.

Bird fanciers stick to a consistent feeding schedule because the birds get used to it and would otherwise be easily prone to health problems. If they find that their feed bins remain empty

at what they think is feeding time, they'll forage around on the ground, picking up contaminated or moldy seeds. Be sure to blow out the empty husks from feeders before adding fresh seeds. Throw away all fruit and greens left over from the day before. Such items are often already rotten though you can't see it

Photo by Dr. Herbert R. Axelrod

An American Yellow color variety of the Peach-faced Lovebird, *Agapornis roseicollis*.

yet. During the breeding season, you may want to fill the feeders in the evening shortly before you turn the lights out. Then the older birds can feed easily in the morning while you are still asleep, and thus they begin feeding the young hours earlier. I've done this often, and frequent feedings during daylight hours benefit the young.

Greens in general are always very important to parrots, and that includes our lovebirds. Our little Africans seem to especially like succulent leaves. Yet, many birds from breeders are not accustomed to greens, which is why the new owner can have difficulty in getting

his birds to take them.

The fancier acts in his own interests by *not* treating his garden greens and fruits with pesticides. In the winter, remember that ice-cold greens are not wholesome, whereas, contrary to common belief, freshly thawed greens won't hurt. However, they rot faster than fresh greens in the summer! Soiled leaves and fruits may have to be rinsed off, and should at least be somewhat dried before being eaten.

Here's a selection of plants just to get your own ideas started: dandelion, chickweed, chickory or endive, carrots, apples, pears, lettuce, and parsley (smooth and curly).

You can bring small amounts of unripe cereal grains like oats, wheat or corn back from summer hikes. Shepherd's purse and *Senecio* may be growing along the edges of the fields. Sod pieces or grassy plots are quite useful in the aviaries. Perhaps you, too, might find it practical and advantageous to set budgerigar feed out in flat bowls or the bottom saucers of flowerpots to germinate and sprout; then put those "freshly grown vegetables" in the cages or enclosures. It is an all-year-round possibility, and you should try it.

Freshly peeled branches of the appropriate deciduous trees and bushes are very useful for gnawing, according to my own 25 years of observations. Lovebirds enjoy this activity very much. Even if the nutritional value of the bark is slight, the sap does have good effects. It has been shown to facilitate the molting process and to brighten the plumage colors.

In the winter, you can try rowan (mountain ash), hawthorne, juniper berries and soaked raisins as supplemental vegetable food. Carrots are available year 'round—scrape them for better taste appeal—and they can be dried and mixed with soft foods.

Aside from seeds and greens, a bird also needs minerals and trace elements, of course. My advice is to ask first what your pet shop has available. There are, for example, mineral-enriched, ultraviolet-irradiated grits, as well as quite a few other calcium preparations on the market. Making your own mineral preparations is difficult and as a rule not worth the effort that it would take even to search for all the ingredients.

Finely ground oyster shell would also be useful, of course, as well as cuttlefish bones. These items contain useful amounts of sea salt, iodine, trace elements and calcium.

Vitamins are indeed useful, but synthetic products can easily give us too much of a good thing. Despite long denial, new findings do indeed show that overdosage causes vitamin poisoning. Once a week (twice in winter) is really enough to add them to feed or water. From long years of experience, I'd like to advise you against adding strong-smelling, vile-tasting or viscous preparations to the drinking water, for most of it will be poured down the drain, because the birds will either refuse to drink or else take to the bathwater.

So-called egg food, the proven mixture of the old guard of canary breeders, it can be used supplementally all year

Photo by Dr. Herbert R. Axelrod

The larger feeders, such as shown here, are not the practical way to feed your lovebird. It is easier but the feed can become stale, or worse yet, only be seed hulls without the meat.

long, although not exactly daily. In general, birds rapidly show a liking for it, which is definitely known to be advantageous in rearing the young birds. With the help of modern kitchen appliances, a large quantity can be mixed up and refrigerated in portion-size amounts. Some poppy seed may enhance the mixture's digestibility.

WAYS TO AVOID FEED WASTAGE

Large feeders to hold nice-looking seed mixtures are not always so practical for general use in lovebird enclosures. Most birds, in their search for their favorite seeds in a mixture, have the habit of scattering about the other ingredients, which often go

bad. Large bowls filled only with a shallow layer are some help. In the final analysis, it depends upon your particular circumstances whether wasted feed can be tolerated. Feed which falls on smooth, and, above all, dry ground or floors can be swept up and passed through an ordinary feed cleaner. The amount of salvaged feed is surprisingly large and may warrant an investment. It's not a bad idea to give the particularly favorite sunflower seeds, which the birds always look for first, in separate containers in large bowls or in flat wooden boxes, which control the wasteful scattering of the bird feed.

The feeding spot should always be the same. When I set up my first aviary, my newly acquired birds almost starved because they weren't used to automatic feeders, and there were not any ordinary feeding receptacles in the enclosure. Speaking of automatic feeders, they are not 100% reliable. According to my own experience, they are never reliable enough for you to be able to go away carefree, without someone who can look in for you while you're on vacation.

One last fundamental thought on feeding ornamental birds: the fact that birds survive and even raise their babies is not necessarily proof that they are optimally kept and fed. No matter how often someone gives me that argument, I still have to realize that the drive of self-preservation and that of reproduction are the greatest drives in nature. All living organisms strive, also under inadequate living conditions, to "stay on top of it," assert themselves, and reproduce. Many bird fanciers should be aware of that. It applies specially to smaller ornamental birds as well, on whose care and feeding one might erroneously try to skimp and save.

DRINKING AND BATH WATER

The importance of clear, clean water, if possible clear of chlorine, not too cold, and given fresh at least once a day, is often underestimated in its effect on health and well being. Don't be misled by any observation that seems to show that lovebirds drink relatively little, for such appearances do not have to be a permanent condition. Fresh water twice a day is recommended for midsummer heat, very warmly heated rooms, or where there's a lot of smoking. Water is best

given in non-rusting receptacles which are placed in such a way so that dust, seed husks, and, above all, bird droppings can't fall into the water. If strong sunlight strikes the water at times during the day, then a greenish black algal growth will occur. Algae produces oxygen and would even keep the water fresh! The disadvantage, however, is that it accumulates dirt particles.

Photo by Dr. Herbert R. Axelrod

This Peach-face is having a great bath. Don't use the same water for drinking that is used for bathing.

If you've ever taken a drink out of a glass which still contained traces of the detergent with which it was washed, then you'll be considerate enough to vigorously rinse your lovebirds' water receptacle. If possible, try to keep your birds from bathing in the drinking receptacles.

Also, for health reasons, the bath water is not for drinking, but that's more difficult to avoid. Supply fresh bath water daily, but only by the hour. Most lovebirds are known to be passionately fond

of bathing. Real cleansing and preening is only possible with a bath, without which there's hardly any really smooth, glossy plumage. Bathing also improves the breeding outlook considerably! Inconvenient and involved tricks for humidifying the inside of the nesting boxes, in my opinion, are largely unnecessary. There are, of course, also water-shy lovebirds, or, more precisely, those who don't quite want to duck under the water. They might, however, like to frollick around in wet grass, a fine spray from a sprinkler, or in a light rain during the warm part of the year.

In cool winds or when the temperature drops in the autumn, however, think twice about outdoor bathing, especially since the birds may not even feel like it. I once operated outdoor baths in the winter, but with warm water, and I found that the birds bathed when it was chilly, and a little later lumps of ice fell from the perch. Don't get the same idea, as obvious as it seems at first glance. Aviary bathing set-ups must necessarily be closed from the end of September until spring (but that varies, of course, depending upon geographical location). Two or three weeks before shutting down, the bird fancier should install water dispensers or something similar at appropriate, protected spots.

Clean bath water is without any doubt an effective and also inexpensive beauty treatment, as well as a necessity for all ornamental birds—especially for parrots! Where the water supply is inadequate as far as avian nutrition goes, whether because of calcium content, acidity, contamination or chemical composition and/or toxicity, bird fanciers have obtained excellent results with different kinds of mineral water. In gaseous mineral waters, the carbonic acid or carbon dioxide gas is allowed to bubble off by shaking the bottle. Mineral water, according to source or bottler, is superbly suitable for close-to-natural supply of minerals and trace elements. Lovebird breeders who have experienced losses due to damaged or cracked eggs are strongly advised to try mineral water. Even mixing it with tap water leads to a somewhat thicker eggshell.

This lovely blue color variety of the Peach-faced Lovebird could cause himself harm if he ingests some of this flower. Keep your pet lovebird away from all house plants to be safe.

Photo by Robert Pearcy

Photo courtesy of Four Paws

Your local pet shop will supply products that will enable you to grow and offer your lovebird fresh home grown greens that are free of pesticides.

Item No. 93112

WILD WALK

12/13" PERCH

Photo courtesy of Finny World Class Pet Products

Unique Nature Design
Great for Bird's Feet & Legs

◆ **Exercises & Strengthens Muscles**
◆ **Helps Reduce Foot & Leg Ailments**
◆ **All Safe, Non-Toxic Materials**
◆ **Adjusts to Various Cage Sizes**

1 Year Warranty*

Made in USA

Photo courtesy of Penn-Plax

Food and water should be readily available for your lovebird. Most cups can be attached right to the cage for easy access.

Photo courtesy of Penn-Plax

A wide variety of bird cages are available at your local pet shop. It is important to purchase a size large enough to comfortably house your lovebird.

Perches are very important to the condition of your bird's feet. Some perches are uniquely designed, varying in contour along their length, allowing the bird to have a number of different diameters to grip.

MASKED LOVEBIRD

AGAPORNIS PERSONATA PERSONATA

The original form of the lovebird with its so-called white eye rings (periorbital ring) is an impressive sight. The German ornithologist Anton Reichnoff was the first to describe this bird. The above mentioned ring around the eye is really a bare, featherless strip of skin, which many of the larger parrots also have. The four lovebird species that possess an eye ring were at first thought to be independent species; geographically they live close together and feed similarly on dry grass seeds on the ground which germinate and sprout into plants only once a year during the rainy season. Even as captive birds in enclosures they behave strikingly alike and in any case do have much in common. The physically largest species and the one after which the others are named (in Latin) will be discussed in detail and then the closely related ones will be described only insofar as they differ or possess their own peculiarities.

One could say that the Masked Lovebirds have long been the most widely kept smaller parrot, and that the storm of enthusiasm for these little Africans is actually increasing. This enthusiasm, of course, refers to the entire group and not to each of the four varieties to the same extent.

The Masked Lovebird has a somewhat aggressive personality. Imported birds have to be carefully accustomed to things, which is true even for those from Japan, which is why birds bred domestically are no doubt the best choice for beginners. While they may not be little cage birds in the ordinary sense, they do keep better in cages than other related birds. Handfed individuals are fine pets and become remarkably tame.

If the birds are kept caged and inside the home all year long, then no nesting/

Agapornis personata personata, the Masked Lovebird.

Photos by Reinhard Tierfoto

The blue hybrid of the Masked Lovebird, *Agapornis personata personata*.

sleeping box is necessary. Free flight opportunity around the room would be very advisable. All wooden objects, however, are in danger. The little fellows are all too happy to nibble and gnaw.

Masked Lovebirds can be kept in flights or aviaries with other lovebirds of either the same species, or of another. It is not advisable to house them with other parrot-like birds such as budgies, cockatiels or Australian parakeets.

The *personata* races or subspecies living in relatively small, adjacent habitats have not ever interbred in the wild. In the aviary, however, they do it readily, which is evidence of their close relationship. Together with the color varieties (mutations) meanwhile being bred, the number of Masked Lovebirds now being kept must be enormous. Not all are purebred, by any means, not even the majority of them, in my estimation. But that doesn't always turn out bad, although the breeder should still strive to breed pure if he can do it.

My attempts to measure a dead bird didn't give any completely reliable values. The living bird, however, doesn't like to be measured, which is the weak link in all measurements reported for birds. The Masked Lovebird is supposed to attain 14.5 to 15.6 cm (5.7 to 6 inches). One wing spread out is supposed to be about 10 to 10.5 cm (3.9 to 4 inches). Visually, however, the wings seem to be short! The bird's weight is about 50 grams (1.8 ounces), with 10% more weight for the heavier female.

Always be sure that the original form described here really has a *yellow* collar beneath the neck or nape and

note that the hen is larger than the cock and seems more powerfully built.

When you have a chance, let an experienced fancier demonstrate sexing by palpation of the pelvic bones. In the female, the distance

darker plumage coloration, especially noticeable on and around the head. There are transitory small black spots on the upper half of the beak, and continuing on back to the base of the beak. The black in the plumage is not yet very dark.

Banding of the progeny is advisable for better identification of individuals. A band can also note the bird's sex once you have any basis for detecting it. Also a daub of color or cutting of specific feathers can indicate a bird's sex.

The first living Masked Lovebirds are supposed to have been taken home by an American explorer in 1925. The first commercial imports to Germany and the rest of Europe began in 1927. Breeding success was immediate: Germany and Switzerland as early as 1928. America, however, protected from the war's devastation, had an enormous headstart in lovebird breeding, including the first color varieties.

Now let's talk about noteworthy characteristics of the Masked Lovebird and its care. These birds are astonishingly passionate water sprites which need continual opportunity to bathe. They drink often and a lot, which the fancier must know and facilitate for them. Furthermore, fresh juicy branches are important for maintenance of health, even before and after the mating season (when branches and twigs are used for nesting material). In my opinion, they're even better than many medications.

There's a great deal to say about keeping an aviary and

A lovely Blue Masked Lovebird, *Agapornis personata personata.*

across the upper chest, and that the whole head to the nape or scruff of the neck is brownish black. Mixed breeds, as already mentioned, are widespread, and mix-ups always occur.

Males and females look completely alike. It's all the better when the seller of breeding pairs agrees to take back any wrongly sexed birds. So it's wise to have an exchange clause in the initial purchase agreement.

Once you have a proven breeding pair of lovebirds in hand, you will often be able to

between both pelvic bones is supposed to be 5 to 7 mm (0.2 to 0.28 inch), whereas the distance in the male is only 1 to 2 mm (0.04 to 0.08 inch).

Anyone who specializes in sexing birds in this manner can really do wonders. But there's no easy formula in it for the average bird fancier. So selecting male and female pairs is, and remains, one of the first difficult hurdles to pass before starting to breed lovebirds.

Young *Agapornis personata personata* have duller and

avoiding unpleasant experiences. Not all Black-Masked Lovebirds are equally inured against cold or moist weather or frosty winter nights. The fleshier a bird's foot and the higher the atmospheric humidity, the more are the chances of frozen feet during the cold season. At night, especially, the Black-Masked Lovebird should be kept in a shelter. If you give them empty nesting boxes, but without any nesting material, the birds will usually keep warm in them without laying any eggs; but there's no guarantee of that, because the mating drive is powerful. When brooding is attempted during the winter, the Masked Lovebird hens suffer more from laying problems than other related kinds of birds. In cool moist summers the same can happen, often in aviaries without shelter. My own experiences indicate that keeping the birds outdoors is safe down near the freezing point. In continuous frost or freezing, however, the birds must either be taken inside your home, or else provided with their own solidly built house.

Wooden parts of the aviary will be nibbled on, however, this could weaken the structure. It is advised to construct a double layering of mesh (one layer on each side of a wooden frame). This will not only protect the wooden framing, but the birds in the adjacent flights as well.

COURTSHIP AND NESTING

In courtship, the cock of this lovebird species is very passive. The hen has to formally signal her mating readiness, and does it by fluffing up her feathers. Have no fear that she's showing a symptom of illness! When the shy cock finally approaches her, she begs to be fed. However, he doesn't accept the invitation in any great hurry, but acts in a

Photo by Michael Gilroy

A Blue Masked Lovebird, *Agapornis personata personata*, chewing on straw. The average Masked Lovebird weighs under two ounces when in perfect condition.

characteristically comical manner, often scratching his head as if he was embarrassed.

All of this doesn't develop as quickly as I've described it. But finally he does feed her, not for long, but rather symbolically, which must be the triggering stimulus. The male can now mount the female. To further encourage the still undecided male, the female ducks down and lets her wings hang down somewhat. The male clumsily climbs up to the female's back, and the actual mating can last several minutes. I can't say, however, that it's the rule, because shorter copulation times of 15 to 20 seconds also occurs. The hen sets the pace, for she can break off this activity whenever she wants to. Otherwise, the male completes the act and climbs down over his mate's head. According to my own observations, only undisturbed, completely consummated matings produce fertile eggs in the nest.

For the actual copulatory act, the male winds his tail around the sharply angled tail of the female, and holds on by firmly biting into her nape plumage. To all appearances,

Two Masked Lovebirds, *Agapornis personata personata*, a yellow hybrid and a blue hybrid.

mating is strenuous, for at least the male seems inactive and visibly exhausted for minutes. The female urges him on with her beak.

With very tame couples who do not mind close observation during mating, you can see the ejaculation of semen into the female's cloaca. This is a useful observation for breeders to make, especially to confirm insemination in newly breeding pairs.

Masked and closely related species of the *personata* group carry nesting material with their beaks into the nesting hollows they select. Slowly but surely a large, domed nest forms, and its floor is likewise padded. You can only frustrate and hinder breeding birds who are engaged in carrying out their mating business if you provide them with nesting sites that are too small.

The breeder can, to a certain extent, control, by the materials he provides, just how long nest-building goes on. According to my frequent "clinical notes," this baby business can last three or four weeks. I can safely say that relatively much more care is expended by the Masked Lovebirds in construction than is usual for the other lovebird species, except perhaps the Grey-headed or Madagascan Lovebird (Ag*apornis cana*), who similarly builds nests as carefully.

Branches, twigs, and shreds of bark are the preferred construction materials. I gather long weeping willow branches; they are the best you can offer the birds. If they are unavailable, then I recommend thin hazelnut branches. Likewise, thin fruit-tree branches would also be suitable.

The lovebirds will skillfully peel off the bark themselves. Willow branches are not only the juiciest, but also retain their moisture the longest. After all of the above discussion, the reader will readily agree that a roomy nesting box contributes significantly to good breeding results. It's best to build it yourself from unplaned boards, about 30 x 30 cm (12 x 12 inches) inside surface and a height which allows at least 35 cm (14 inches) clearance above. The entrance of the nesting box should be 5 to 6 cm (2 to 2.5 inches) across. A nesting box like that made of 15 to 18 stout boards is naturally of substantial weight. Because the tenants fly against it often and heftily, the breeder has to make sure it's absolutely secured. I always use two bolts or fasteners.

It becomes relatively difficult to look inside the nesting box to see what's happening, because the entrance hole side is used as the back wall of the nest. The hen reaches the actual brooding spot by making a 180 degree turn; daylight is almost completely excluded. The way to facilitate visual inspections is not to hang the nesting box higher than you can reach it comfortably while standing on the ground. Only inexperienced beginners climb around on stools or ladders in the aviary. Never do that! Or at least, if necessary, not in the breeding season, and without any birds in the aviary. In addition, I recommend placing the nesting box in the upper left of the aviary, and providing a short, rounded perch (a dowel) about 8 cm (3 inches) below it. The cock, especially, will enjoy perching on it. There's hardly any objection, however, to also providing little landing platforms under the nesting box.

It's mainly the hen who handles nest construction. After her brood has hatched successfully, she might even go out again to look for construction materials. I tend to believe that a few twigs or branches should be provided now. I have frequently found, in all the general housecleaning of heavily used lovebird breeding boxes I've done, that droppings are covered over and hidden by this continual piling up of nesting materials. The birds have often enough buried infertile eggs or dead nestlings under this carpet, and I've later come across their mummified remains. So this drive to carry in more nesting material does have a purpose.

The male guards the nursery, but not quite seriously. If another Masked Lovebird hen wanted to take over the nesting box—and such attempts unfortunately occur from time to time in a breeding colony—he's quite capable of just letting her do so.

Six-month-old birds are already headed for mating. You've got to be ready for

that! Hang up more nesting boxes to keep peace with the increasing number of couples ready to mate. (That's an important secret of successful breeding, which breeders like to keep to themselves.) My own formula is seven nesting boxes for every three pairs of lovebirds.

You can provide a fine-spray fountain or some similar bathing arrangements in the breeding enclosure; then you don't have to worry about all the many tricks recommended for humidifying the nesting boxes. Many of those tricks which are propagated are not only ridiculous but also troublesome and time-consuming.

In Africa, all Masked Lovebirds in the wild reportedly lay up to eight eggs. Four to five white eggs is the usual clutch in captive

breeding. During laying time, the female's droppings are occasionally loose, like diarrhea, but this is normal and usually clears up on its own.

The serious lovebird breeder doesn't count the brooding days but simply waits. I soon stopped taking notes, because there proved to be considerable variation. I believe the average was 23 days. It's an advantage that Masked Lovebird hens settle down to brood after the fourth egg, which is why the young hatch more or less simultaneously, avoiding any often disadvantageous age and size differences in the nest. Surprises, however, pop up more often with the first captive hens.

The first clutch of the new breeding season is often infertile. The breeder can do little about it as long as the

A pair of Masked Lovebirds, *Agapornis personata personata*. The female is in the foreground.

Photo by Arend van den Nieuwenhuizen

reason is not too early a start in a still too cool spring.

Now and again you'll find dead embryos in the egg. It goes without saying that I, too, am aware that death in the egg is supposed to be caused by too little humidity. But at least I'll refrain from resuscitating this theory once again. I certainly don't object to each reader and even my author colleague having his own opinion, but my conviction is firm. The breeder should not be tempted by one of the numerous methods of increasing humidity; the advice to spray the nesting box with the garden hose is, in my opinion, nonsense. Don't put any moist sponges in the lower part of the nesting box, where quite clever fellows have even built water receptacles. The result of all this tampering is, I believe, almost always more disadvantageous than to let things run their natural course. Constant opportunity for the breeding lovebird to bathe is, I believe, enormously important. I used the above mentioned fountain with collecting basin which you can buy ready-made or a trough with continually fresh flowing water.

The cock participates temporarily in brooding the eggs. He is usually astonishingly involved psychologically (if we can say that for a lovebird) in the mating process, and, for example, gets very excited when his offspring crawl out of their eggshells. Unfortunately, it often happens that one brood is not yet ready to fly off, or else clambers back at night into the nest where new eggs have

already been laid. And that's why you need a lot of room!

In colony breeding, I've seen how older birds chase and peck at the young of other couples. Masked Lovebirds are not bred completely devoid of any problems, although their breeding can still unequivocally be considered simple.

Let's talk more about the development of young birds. The need for drinking water increases sharply as the nestling grows. The breeder must absolutely be aware of that and take it into consideration. I am surprised that I keep right on running into even experienced breeders who have not realized it.

The very young nestlings are covered with orange-colored down. Thus the nestlings of Blue Black-masked Lovebirds can show at best pale pink fluff, but usually only white down. That means you can differentiate varieties even in the nest, and such knowledge is of great value to the breeder of color varieties, who must reckon with mixed offspring.

The eyes of the young lovebirds open about the tenth day of life. As soon as you have newborns in the nesting box, I strongly recommend taking a walk, with a pair of scissors, to collect wild grass-seed heads, which are an excellent rearing food I've never omitted, and they don't cost anything, either.

By the end of the third week of life, the quills of the large feathers start coming through the skin. The young Masked Lovebirds leave the

nesting box for the first time in about 44 to 47 days and are fed for about 14 days out in the perch. Young color variety lovebirds almost always "fly the coop" a few days too early. Which is an increased risk, because they always turn out to be somewhat weaker. If you can't manage to check regularly on your breeding spots, you'll suffer considerable losses where you no longer expect them. Questions on this subject from breeders lead me to assume that these causes and effects are not even recognized.

Also I've often found that the feet of young Masked Lovebirds that have just left the breeding boxes are still too weak to hold the birds all night on a thin rounded perch. They finally fall off, and if it's the rainy season or if it rains hard overnight, then they're lost in the garden aviary. As a safeguard, provide perching strips about one-inch wide; put one of them temporarily close to the floor. If the fancier or breeder overlooks any particularly courageous youngster who has already left the nursery, then that bird often enough pays with its life for its precociousness. By itself, it can't find the feeder, and usually can't even eat by itself anyway. The parents feed only the nestmates who have remained in the nest. The choice for the owner is now between putting the nestling back in its nest, or feeding it by hand. As a breeder, make particular effort to see that all the little Masked Lovebirds don't fly out for the first time on the same day, if you can prevent it. In breeding units and cages, the danger is not so great. On the other hand, in such cramped space, if the parents are ready to mate again, they may pursue and bite the offspring.

I'm often asked what rearing feed I give my birds. There's a choice between commercially available prepared products, an egg feed like canary breeders use, and soft mixes from the pet shop. I've preferred to give the prepared feeds ever since they became available. The precondition, however, is that the breeding pair be accustomed to it in time. It is improbable that they'll immediately take a liking to any unknown food.

Young Masked Lovebirds, just as *Agapornis* birds of smaller build, are banded with bands having an inside diameter of 4.5 mm (0.18 inches). Many years ago, an experienced bird fancier advised me to band *both* feet, one with a closed band and one with an open band, which is meant to be removed later. Both bands should be dipped into non-toxic black paint, which should be, of course, completely dry before use. By following this advice, there was actually a noticeable decrease in injuries and instances of a young banded birds being thrown out of the nesting box, for the parents want to remove foreign bodies, but it apparently never occurs

to them that their youngsters are attached to them. This extra banding, of course, makes even more work.

If the young Masked Lovebirds are chased around, bitten by parents who are getting steamed up for new mating activity, then put the young into a metal cage from

Photo by Dr. Herbert R. Axelrod

A Blue Masked Lovebird in excellent condition.

the front of which two perches jut out 10 cm (3.9 inches). Hang this cage in the enclosure, and if it's an older model, remove two or three wires so that the young birds can poke their heads through. The breeder should definitely try this, for the parents come to their senses and remember to feed their begging, screaming babies—who are right there staring them in the face.

MUTATIONS AND THEIR CAUSES

The principles of heredity for numerous budgerigar color variations likewise apply to the lovebirds. The green factor, that is, the wild coloration, is dominant (expresses itself) as a rule. If you read of an offer of, say, green/blue birds, then that means that the green is visible, but the blue, although indeed present as a heredity factor, has not manifested itself. Color breeding, despite the production overtime involved, is advisable only in breeding boxes which can guarantee the proper mating. The art of breeding involves not so much the "invention" of a new mutation or coloration (which occasionally happens by itself anyway with some luck) but more an understanding of how to genetically fix or keep those naturally occurring flukes or capers of Mother Nature. The slightest error in subsequent matings often ruins all chances of a new line. To my great disappointment, it also happened to me. Mutations also occur in the wild, but they rarely breed true, that is, keep on occurring in the offspring. Abnormally colored birds are bitten to death by others of their kind, ostracized from the flock, or if too conspicuous, rapidly fall victims to birds of prey. Only in the breeder's enclosure can something permanent develop.

Even a fixed color mutation, however, can disappear if it is not, so to speak, replenished at more or less regular intervals by inbreeding, which is particularly true for the attractive Blue Black-masked Lovebirds.

An excellent article by a lovebird breeder colleague of mine (Bernhardt, Az-Nachrichten November, 1979) discussed the application of hereditary formula to Masked Lovebirds according to budgerigar hereditary formulas presupposes that the breeding birds don't carry any "mixed blood" (really genes). On the other hand, all these factors must be taken into consideration, and who wants to understand them all in detail? All lovebird species with a white eye ring interbreed, and the Masked Lovebird even interbreeds with *Agapornis roseicollis* (Peach-faced or Rosy-faced Lovebird).

The first blue mutation is supposed to have been brought from Africa in 1927. In 1932 the first blue ones were hatched in France. Today, most Blue Black-masked Lovebirds grow up in California breeding aviaries. They attract a lot of attention in the pet trade and reproduce well, but have to be kept warm in winter. There are naturally various opinions as to their attractiveness. Genetically, the blue mutation is autosomal recessive.

Shortly after World War II, a Mr. Rudkin was responsible for certainly thousands of the lovebirds in stock and out in the public. He began in the mid-1930s, and by the end of the war in 1945 had reached the pinnacle of success, while all stock in Europe had been annihilated. Thanks to his

efforts, the going price then in the U.S for Blue-masked Lovebirds was lower than the price of imported birds. That could really make a European envious.

It was in California, too, that the first recessive Yellow Masked Lovebirds appeared in 1935. You can still see the natural blue, although very dilute, in some features, and the dusky melanin pigmentation. Just as in budgerigars, other colors can be bred, such as, for example, by combination matings of independent color varieties (mutations). Thus, breeders in Japan created birds which appeared to be whitish, but which kept the black on the head. When the sunlight strikes these novel creations, you can see that they are really cool blue, that is, white with a bluish shimmer. In the mid-1950s, the bird zoo and dealer *Animali* in Eindhoven, the Netherlands, advertised such Far East novelty imports a great deal. I even took a trip there to have a look at the wonder birds myself. I was certainly impressed, but I felt no impulse to buy this mutation. That was lucky for me, because the sudden flash-in-the-pan interest soon subsided. There also once appeared a completely white Masked Lovebird without any mask, for whatever attractiveness that's supposed to offer. Danish parrot fanciers, by the way, really know about novel breeds and varieties.

Other color varieties of the Masked Lovebird have shown up: white-blue, yellow with greenish shimmer, cinnamon, piebald (pied harlequin), and buttercup or lutino. Likewise, the yellow of a natural orange-

red coloration can be intensified, which can be quite pretty.

The more breeders that turn their attention to lovebirds, the sooner the probability will increase that we'll be able to look forward to even more color varieties.

The Masked Lovebird is highly recommended for beginners in lovebird breeding, and it is now growing in popularity. My advice to the beginner is to start right off breeding with several pairs. Let each pair breed twice a year, or perhaps three times a year, later when dealing with tried and proven breeding pairs. Always aim at maintaining your breeding birds in the best of health, well nourished and optimally cared for. But don't grieve for losses among the newborn, for not even the leading expert can avoid them. Self-recrimination is only appropriate if you've been negligent and failed through your own fault. In any case, you can do it better next time.

If we consider the whole relatively small African group of lovebirds, then the Masked Lovebird is doubtless the second (to the Peach-faced or Rosy-faced lovebird) favorite species in the world. The lines of natural-colored Masked Lovebirds are still healthy and robust. The lines of the color varieties, on the other hand, could probably make good use of an intensive genetic replenishment. The blue x blue cross, a particular favorite because it yields only blue offspring, rapidly ruins the good condition of this favorite color variety. A certain amount of know-how is necessary for the successful breeding of birds.

The Masked Lovebird, *Agapornis personata personata*. This prized photo was taken by Horst Mueller of Braunschweig using a Novoflex camera with Anscochrome films.

by Dr. Herbert R. Axelrod

In wonderful condition, this champion normally colored Masked Lovebird, Agapornis personata personata, is photographed on a piece of petrified cactus

BLACK-CHEEKED LOVEBIRD

AGAPORNIS PERSONATA NIGRIGENIS

If you want to determine the essential differences between the Masked Lovebirds and Black-cheeked Lovebirds, then look at the body size and the original form, *Agapornis personata personata,* with its yellow chest, neck/nape plumage, for it is not uncommon for the Black-cheeked and Masked to be confused with one another. The plumage of the smaller Black-cheeked Lovebird is green at those spots however similar it may seem when both of these related lovebirds are seen together. The eye ring is the common characteristic. There are differences in weight: an adult Black-cheeked Lovebird weighs 40 grams (1.4 ounces) at the most, and particularly stout females can weigh an additional 5 grams (0.18 ounce). Black-cheeked Lovebirds give the impression of being especially elegant and graceful.

These little parrots first reached Europe alive in 1908. It can hardly be explained why they were neither too much in demand, nor achieved even average distribution, nor reproduced in the hands of fanciers. Even today, getting one probably takes a little longer than acquiring others. We're speaking here, of course, of purebred specimens. It does perturb me to have to admit that in breeding today, the desired genetic purity is hardly the rule. That's an unhappy state of affairs, particularly when unsuspecting purchasers are taken in with the offspring of such poor breeding practices.

The wild Masked Lovebird's natural distribution is limited today to a very small region in what was formerly Northern Rhodesia (now Zimbabwe), where for many years the

The Black-cheeked Lovebird, *Agapornis personata nigrigenis* which is often simply referred to as *Agapornis nigrigenis.*

natives set out bird lime along whole forest edges and near fields of ripening millet in order to get rid of pests which were destroying their crops. Their "success" in many places became seriously close to annihilation of the birds. Today, the Black-cheeked Lovebird is considered to be the first lovebird to be on the endangered bird list! These attractive little African parrots were known and in demand among European bird fanciers before WWI but the subsequent economic collapse wreaked much havoc.

This first peak importation of short duration was followed in England only by a second period after 1927 to about the mid-1950s. As you see, the depletion of stock was essentially slowed down, yet it remains unexplained historically just how on two occasions initially high stocks of birds fell almost to zero again. One can say that the Black-cheeked Lovebird as a pet for parrot fanciers almost perished twice.

In 1945, when all Europe lay in the rubble of war, the wild lovebirds in Rhodesia were almost wiped out, for in the chaos of war no one had the time or inclination to worry about controlling private annihilation campaigns. It is to the greater glory of the British colonial administration of that time to have stopped the wholesale extermination at the last moment. Just how the new masters of the land consider natural conservation is very uncertain.

Europe's lovebird fanciers have come to the depressing conclusion that all the good opportunities for the breeding of lovebirds by fanciers have never been significantly exploited. The Japanese promptly seized the opportunity. While we let Black-cheeked Lovebirds disappear, individual breeders bastardized what was left over often enough with *Agapornis lilianae* (Nyasa or Nyasaland Lovebirds) or *Agapornis personata personata* (Masked Lovebirds). Mixed-breed birds weren't always obvious, and the outward appearance of the Black-cheeked Lovebird dominates. That doesn't make any difference, because such genetically split mixed breeds are unequivocally second rate. The parrot expert DeGrahl advises us always to consider birds with a black head, pure yellow throat or blue uppertail coverts as mixed breeds.

If someone wanted to purposely set about to help the attractive Black-cheeked Lovebird survive in bird fanciers' aviaries, a group of genetically pure wild specimens would first have to be imported. Perhaps some organizationally talented idealist will seize this chance, because it might be the last one.

Why does this cute little creature arouse so little interest in us? Keeping as well as breeding them is rather rewarding, and their care and feeding are not difficult. Indeed, one could be justified in praising the Black-cheeked Lovebird as the most lovable of the lovebirds, at least as far as a companion for human beings goes. Moreover, community accommodations with other ornamentals in spacious aviaries would be without any losses. Likewise, many breeders have succeeded in keeping several breeding pairs housed together in a colony without any great difficulty. All of that indicates relatively little aggression. Furthermore, patient bird fanciers achieve astonishingly good results in taming and training the Black-cheeked Lovebird.

The first ones were already bred in aviaries, according to British sources, a year after they were originally imported. The greatest number of birds hatched was supposed to have been achieved in Britain in 1909, and in only two broods. The greatest number of broods per year amounted to five, in warm climates.

Photo by Vogelspark Walsrode

The lovely Black-cheeked Lovebird has not been one of hobbyists favorite varieties of lovebird for some unknown reason.

If we want to achieve our own breeding success, although certainly somewhat more modest, let's first clear the hurdle of differentiating the sexes. If you start with healthy pairs that get along together, then offspring will be produced reliably and regularly. Black-cheeked Lovebirds make very good parents. In addition, after getting acclimated, they are amazingly resistant to the weather, including the ability to tolerate considerable fluctuation in temperature. I'm convinced that Black-cheeked Lovebirds can tolerate moderate frost or freezing surprisingly well for short periods, but despite that, it is not advisable to

expose them to subzero temperatures more than three hours daily. They belong in the safety of the birdhouse even before sunset. It can be risky, too, if the fancier lets his flock out in the cold before he leaves for work early in the morning. Even perches coated with frost can freeze the birds' feet, which later adversely affects the male's ability to mate.

Of all the members of the genus *Agapornis* which are available today, the elegant Black-cheeked Lovebird is the best cagebird or "parlor bird." Understand this fact, however, in the sense that life in a cage for many of this bird's relatives described in this book is under duress, can lead to fits, apathy, depression, health disorders and early death. Therefore, attempts to breed the Black-cheeked Lovebirds, too, in flight cages, or small indoor aviaries can be advised, whereby the more numerous progeny, at good prices, would find takers for years to come. At the same time, such increased breeding would be good for maintenance of the species.

There are a few little problems in breeding, and the only reason they have not yet been adequately explained is because the interest and exchange of experience associated with such small stock has remained so minimal. The not uncommon observation comes to mind here that in heavily populated aviaries, a few eggs are infertile from the very start. Likewise, a certain proportion of developing embryos die in the eggshell before hatching. If more Black-cheeked Lovebirds were kept, such problems could probably be resolved merely by the publication of breeding reports and by discussion among breeders.

The deaths of embryos referred to above, which for decades, without exception, were blamed on insufficient moisture in the nesting boxes, does actually occur more rarely in garden aviaries than indoors where drier air predominates; that can, of course, be seen as an indictment. African explorers reported that Black-cheeked Lovebirds in the wild stayed conspicuously in the vicinity of waterfalls, for example on the Zambesi river or at Victoria Falls. They were seen to bathe amply there in the morning and once again in late afternoon. It's certainly advisable to provide continual bathing opportunity where possible, which is guaranteed to promote breeding success. I am even rather convinced that lovebird breeders can spare themselves, in this simple way, all the inconvenient arrangements for artificially humidifying the nesting boxes, for the female most assuredly is still wet from her bath when she sets herself down to brood.

The reader should not interpret the above to mean that Black-cheeked Lovebirds are problem birds insofar as their reproduction is concerned. They are not only good, reliable parents, but once they have decided on

mating, they do it rapidly and resolutely. The clutch consists of up to seven eggs. Most of the time, the female broods, with the male relieving her at times, but only for short stretches. Brood times of 16 to 26 days have been reported. As is often the case, the

An old drawing of a Black-cheeked Lovebird, *Agapornis nigrigenis*, by the famed bird artists Eric Peake.

breeder can hardly estimate exactly when an ongoing brooding session really begins. With Black-cheeked Lovebirds, we can't use an otherwise conspicuous indicator—the male is bringing his brooding mate food—because in this case he does it only irregularly.

The average brooding duration may be 22 or 23 days. Both parents again participate in parenthood now, and feed their successfully hatched babies. With the best feeding, the nestlings grow up and take off on their first flight from the nursery into the enclosure when they're 33 to 36 days old.

There may be some problem now and then as a result of the intervals at which the potentially numerous nestlings hatch. Without fail, there will now be differences in growth and development, and thus differences in the ability to stretch up and open wide to beg for food. It's unavoidable here, as among all bird species with numerous offspring, that some of the little parrot-beaked babies will perish.

I've often liked to discuss with parrot experts the obvious question of why being rare, in demand, and such a favorite of parrot fanciers never did much for the Black-cheeked Lovebird. How can you explain that the majority of successful Black-cheeked Lovebird breeders know how to remain successful at bird shows for only a few years? We come to the conclusion that because of rarity and demand, good breeding pairs are overburdened, and all offspring which make it to the perching stage, including all the prize-winners, are turned into money. The buyers are hardly helped with any advice on how next to proceed, for who wants to turn to the competitors for help? So the evidence is that no continuous development of a breed line can occur. Resolutions and plans to keep the best specimens among the offspring for one's own breeding program are happily forgotten when offers run high. One day, however, there's a set-back—sickness or deaths, or a line reaches the end of its fertile span.

The unpleasantly surprised owner is faced with the question of whether he should start all over again from the beginning; he now has no other choice. As I know breeder mentality, he'll only do that in rare cases, but will notify his colleagues that he has long since been wanting to start with other species, and has now procured or added this and that . . . After all, who wants to admit to his own planning mistakes? These are the difficult-to-understand cases in which a more or less well-known specialist and expert disappears from the show programs from one year to the next, at the same time drying up a source of new birds for other breeders. I've gone a little astray here in our discussion just to bring out how relatively easy it would be to still reverse this downhill trend. The attractive Black-cheeked Lovebird is not to blame, however, for his repeated downfalls in numbers.

The same goes for the color varieties which people complain are missing, and which give such high value to a few relatives. How could they possibly exist as long as the numbers of stock birds

remain so much below normal? Much could be achieved if serious efforts were made. You hear of yellow (lutinos) and piebalds (or pieds or harlequins), but few people have ever seen such varieties. Do the Japanese intend to surprise the fanciers? Japanese exports reach significant levels in the U.S.A., and from acquaintances in California I received an enthusiastic description of the attractive colors, robust constitution and genetically pure-breeding qualities of these imports.

After four years' attentive observation of Far-eastern successes in animal breeding, I don't believe that we could achieve anything similar. German bird fanciers resist viewing bird production as a commercial enterprise, although financial considerations are acceptable to cover the costs of the hobby. Nevertheless, we could do ourselves a favor and correct decades of mistakes.

Where is a colleague who wants to travel, has experience in Africa and ability to negotiate, and who'll get for us one last, guaranteed genetically pure lot of birds and accompany this import shipment to an overseas airport? Distribution would have to be planned, of course, to include subsequent purposeful and concerted efforts.

If a club or study group took over the coordination of the aforementioned efforts, then the experts could certainly re-establish new lines. Who knows whether these endangered lovebirds might one day soon survive only as an aviary bird? People

have often enough sadly complained to me that the days of great deeds in the bird fanciers' world are all past, and how could they still make a name for themselves today.

I'd like to suggest that the beginners gain their first breeding experience with lovebirds of the most domesticated species. Experience is necessary because the Black-cheeked Lovebird male frequently attacks the fledglings who have already flown out, but who are not yet completely independent, and so these have to be fed by hand. That's all the more difficult because young lovebirds, even those so large, are at first terribly fearful of us and our doings. In the hands of the irresolute and faint-hearted, they would be lost at the last moment.

I don't know what the import situation will be when you read this book, but I don't want to discourage any bonafide bird lovers who really want to keep these little, droll, short-tailed fellows at home. Where taming exercises, family involvement, and free flight are planned for inside, both parties are magnificently served. Possessing birds which are relatively seldom seen is not fun. So, among other concrete advantages, many bird fanciers go to the extra expense of, so to speak, building their home around the birds. Whether you've acquired a real breeding pair is not so important as long as they get along well together. The main thing is to have at least two lovebirds in the set-up.

If one of the two birds dies, you may have a serious problem. An enlightened

Photo by Mueller-Schmida

Black-cheeked Lovebirds, *Agapornis nigrigenis,* make wonderful pets but they are very difficult to find at your local pet shop. Perhaps they can be ordered for you through your local bird supplier?

specialist can no longer take the concept of inseparable so literally, although the grief of the survivor was genuine in at least ten instances I observed in various lovebird species, including the Black-cheeked Lovebird. (Remember, the German and the French names for lovebirds are translated into English as the *inseparables*.) This does not mean that the first bird you introduce into the cage as a new mate will automatically be accepted. The pair must be monitored for a few days to ensure that no fighting will occur.

When lovebirds are involved in any indoor aviary plans, a knowledgeable pet dealer who advises us honestly will recommend only Black-cheeked Lovebirds. Seldom, however, is he in a position to do so, because he doesn't know where to obtain them. May the ongoing rapidly increasing enchantment with these little African parrots take a turn for the best in this respect, too.

FISCHER'S LOVEBIRD

AGAPORNIS PERSONATA FISCHERI

Fischer's Lovebirds are perhaps the most frequently kept species of lovebirds. Most lovebird fanciers, in any case, consider it the most attractive.

Although Fischer's Lovebirds sell nicely abroad, they are vigorously persecuted in their native Africa because of the severe damage they do to crops, fruit and cereal grain, including corn. Looking ahead, the South Africans have established large breeding farms on which huge aviaries, set up in a natural breeding colony system, house 50 to 100 pairs and are very productive. Large colony breeding is feasible, although it has often been disputed.

Even if imported birds are supposed to be available in the animal trade, I still advise beginners to acquire locally bred birds. Risks are thus considerably reduced, and, in addition, change of locality is stressful for the birds.

Even beginners can try their hand at breeding. After earlier generations of breeders have applied themselves to elucidate the ways and means, one only has to follow the guidelines which have already been worked out, and also to have some breeder's good luck.

Fischer's Lovebird is not too suitable for keeping in a cage; if it has to be, then only temporarily. I simply had to do it for several winters. I can say that the fancier will do well to modify the feed so as to prevent the Fischer's getting fat during the time its freedom of movement is sharply curtailed in the cage. As far as is practical, reduce the proportion of fat-rich seeds such as niger, hemp, nuts, large sunflower seeds, etc. Unfortunately, there are cases such as the one in which I myself was taken aback and had to stand helplessly by while Fischer's Lovebirds from a large aviary became melancholic when transferred to a cage. Now and then, in such cases, you've got to reckon with death due to psychic causes.

There is no problem in getting domesticallyn bred Fischer's Lovebirds. Lovebird clubs or the advertisements in fanciers' magazines are very helpful. Meanwhile pet shop stocks are increasing.

Fischer's Lovebirds grow to about 15 cm (6 inches), with one wing outstretched (that is, half a wing spread) of about 9 cm (3.5 inches). Males weigh about 46 to 48 grams (1.6 to 1.7 ounces) when fully grown. Females can weigh 50 to 52 grams (1.8 to 1.9 ounces). Since determination of sex is as much a problem as it is in the original form (*Agapornis personata*, the Masked Lovebird), and since I went into detail as to possibilities and methods of determination in that section, I refer the reader to those pages. Another possibility in the case of Fischer's Lovebirds is that the males only rarely show any interest in fully checking out the interiors of newly hung nesting boxes.

Birds which do that are, in all probability, females.

Whoever buys guaranteed breeding pairs is not necessarily as guaranteed as he thinks he is. They not uncommonly begin to decline in fertility and breeding performance, and that's when the previous owner wants to give them up. So pay attention, as much as possible, to the age recorded on the leg ring. Any breeding birds older than four years at the most are no bargain, even if their sexes are guaranteed. With particularly attractive specimens, however, an exception may seem to be in order. What was said earlier about the coloration of immature Masked Lovebirds also applies to Fischer's Lovebird, except that the beak in immature Fischer's Lovebirds is marbled or mottled brownish. Adults don't show any differences between the sexes, if one doesn't consider, as it just so happens, that the female shows the typical coloration more intensively, particularly the reds. In most other birds, the male is the more attractive and colorful.

Reichnoff named *Agapornis fischeri* after its co-discoverer Dr. G.A. Fischer, who led an expedition to Lake Victoria. The new discovery came almost at the same time as the Masked Lovebird arrived in Europe, from where it was also exported to the U.S.A. This lovebird's eager willingness to reproduce itself in captivity greatly astonished all parrot fanciers. The Berlin

Photo by Horst Bielfeld

Fischer's Lovebird, *Agapornis p. fischeri* may be the most popular of all lovebird species.

Zoo was very successful in breeding them in the early 1930s, where dozens of young Fischer's Lovebirds grew up well. However, the extensive destruction in Europe caused by WWII set parrot breeding back to square one, you might say. I remember quite well that the fanciers' stock of *Agapornis fischeri* was the first to be re-established relatively fast and to increase. Indeed, as early as 1949–1950, I was one of the first buyers.

Flocks and brooding colonies are the usual way of life in their native Africa. Their nesting habits resemble those of the Gray-headed or Madagascan Lovebird (*Agapornis cana*). The reported natural clutch size of ten eggs must be exagggerated. Fischer's Lovebirds (and the Germans, too, call him *Fischeri*, in preference to the German name of Peach-head) are comparatively loud. Their shrill whistles and high-pitched twittering can be heard rather far away and even by people passing in automobiles. I consider this species louder than the Masked Lovebird, but I haven't even found it unpleasant. Neighbors, however, may have another opinion.

I still find it remarkable that Fischer's Lovebirds are such hearty, genial eaters. They need and take a lot of time to feed. Besides seed mixtures, they like two or three fresh branches or twigs and grass seed panicles or wild plants every other day. My birds were crazy about commercially bought cookie-like biscuits softened in milk.

If you want to get on with trying to breed birds, then obtain fully adult specimens in typical coloration from a reputable breeder. Other birds could easily still be too young. If you own an aviary, then the best method for wintering is to bring the birds inside into a sort of bird room, which could also be improvised in a bright, airy basement. In this way, the birds stay in lively spirits and don't show any noticeable disruption in brooding condition when they're later returned to the outside aviary.

The tolerance/tolerability of Fischer's Lovebirds is really quite good if you compare them with other, related species. Two pairs can live together and brood absolutely harmoniously in a large unit with a volume of at least two cubic meters (2.6 cubic yards = 70.6 cubic feet).

Now here's something you should heed, since I'm not afraid of passing on breeding secrets: the breeder who sold me my first expensive breeding pair of lovebirds gave me the good advice that their health and well-being could be interpreted from the red coloration of their beak. If the redness becomes conspicuously paler, then something is definitely wrong with the bird and it will possibly fall ill or fail to breed. I often found that advice confirmed over the next 25 years.

However, only the keeper of several specimens can make use of this color indicator, because he has other birds against which to compare.

During periods of particular physical stress, such as during the second brood, after moving, or in cold weather, it's a good idea to supplement the diet with protein-rich budgerigar tidbits, which are available in pet shops. The protein content of regular lovebird food may be inadequate during severe stress.

Adult Fischer's Lovebirds have long since stopped having a breeding season in Germany. So, the breeder must decide what's good for his charges. Definitely not in the winter! Important tip: with this species of lovebird, inbreeding is less objectionable than with others. That's just something learned by experience, and I don't know why.

Nesting boxes should be roomy if at all possible, as was discussed for the Masked Lovebird. Again, that's dictated by experience; perhaps a particularly spacious interior is good because both parents often enough spend the night together inside with the young. Nest-building became more and more negligent during the course of increasing domestication. I've often observed how at first an irrationally high ground layer is laid down, one which takes away up to 15 cm (6 inches) of space. Roofing, on the other hand, is often merely token. The breeding pairs are provided early on with freshly collected branches and twigs at the height of their succulence for nest-building. They strip off the bark themselves, but every spring I found it appropriate to cut a piece of bark loose with a kitchen knife in order to give them the idea of doing it themselves.

I don't find shredded paper any good for building material. There's not much stability, it molds rapidly, and toxic inks on printed paper can even lead to digestive disturbances. Checking of the nests, as long as it's not overdone, will be calmly accepted by Fischer's

where they come from, as common eggs. Despite advanced domestication, such a procedure is apparently too unnatural, and is not in harmony with the normal behavior of the birds. If all their young hatch on the same day—and that was one

feeding process must proceed slowly as is the rule in the wild.

The best breeding conditions consist of a group of four to eight pairs in constant visual contact, but separated from one another by glass or wire mesh. That

Photo by M.M.Vriends

Agapornis personata fischeri, usually simply called *Agapornis fischeri*, are hearty, genial feeders which consume large amounts of many different kinds of seeds and branches every day!

Lovebirds. This species does not react negatively by being shy or by abandoning the nest eggs. One should never get the idea (although it may seem logical) of collecting the individual eggs and later replacing them, regardless of

of my most interesting experiments—then the parents for some reason, feed only two and let the others starve. I'm very proud of this research result in the style of Helmut Hampe, and am of the opinion, therefore, that the

can perhaps be done, for example, with light-weight separators put into place temporarily.

There's still a certain agitation in the enclosure because Fischer's males like to flirt with strange females who don't have to be their own kind.

Other lovebirds of the opposite sex at the separating wall, however, inflame their passions even more. Even stout budgerigar hens can temporarily join the flock. Mirrors, too, hung up on the outside of the cage can fire up the mating drive.

Clutches range in size from three to six eggs. Five eggs are the usual number, although young hens start with fewer. A day can be skipped between the laying of new eggs. Unfortunately, the hens sit tight and brood often enough right after the first egg. It's not hard to imagine just how irregularly the young will hatch! I've noted that the brooding period runs scarcely three and a half weeks, but I've never counted the days. Both parents begin with the feeding as soon as the first hatchling crawls out of its shell. If this eagerness falters, however, then the owner has a problem. Such cases, unfortunately, are known. Even the very young hens often feed their young poorly or abandon the half-developed chicks for good.

Young Fischer's Lovebirds often fly out in 35 to 37 days, and get feeding help from their parents out in the enclosure for only 11 to 12 days. So they're rather fast growers.

If you've not had any luck in your selection of a breeding pair, then you could find yourself trying to breed a poor line, with physically underdeveloped young which leave the nest while their plumage is not as fully developed as the average bird. If the weather is still cold and rainy at the time, deaths will hardly be avoidable. But, on the other hand, if underdeveloped youngsters like these do well in good weather until they become fully independent, then help them along with rich feed. I've always done that in such cases for the birds' sake so they get a chance at life.

However, I believe I've found that, outwardly, such wretched lovebird babies completely recover and there are no telltale signs. Yet it's not uncommon for them to be a disappointment if they're bred, or if they're sold as such. Therefore, just to be certain, exclude from further breeding any pair which produces weak babies. I know that sounds cruel and unfeeling, but perhaps there is a deficiency in crop mucus or simply abnormal genetics involved.

It's really surprising that such a frequently bred ornamental bird doesn't come in more color varieties. However, the number of wild birds captured was always large and mutations occur much more rarely in such "fresh" imports from the wild.

Bastardization was being carried out quite some time ago, and was successful in producing even more richly colored mixed breeds. Crosses were made even with Blue Masked Lovebirds. Blue Fischer's and lutino Fischer's Lovebirds were developed, then disappeared again. Yellow, yellow-green and whitish birds are still being bred today.

The majority of the different color varieties of Fischer's Lovebird confirms that the life expectancy of these varieties is less than that of the birds with natural coloration. Shortly before the WWII, there was a lot of talk about yellow Fischer's Lovebirds, but my pocket money as a student would never have been enough for such valuables. Yellow birds with red heads were first developed in the early 1930s and are showing up again in modest numbers at the moment.

In 1958—1959, the U.S. market saw large numbers of blue Fischer's Lovebirds. They were somewhat smaller than the normal one and had a whitish-blue head. It seemed appropriate to assume that Blue Masked Lovebirds were inbred. Dr. Burkard is supposed to have bred isabel or fawn birds in Switzerland. Pied or variegated coloration doesn't always seem to be transmitted to offspring.

Those who are interested in color breeding can perhaps obtain heterozygous birds with yellow in their genetic make-up. Although Mendelian laws still apply, it's naturally a matter of chance whether you get what you want from one brood; percentages of results are based upon each 100 birds born. If a Fischer's lovebird heterozygous for yellow is mated with a normal bird, the laws of Mendel predict 50% heterozygous and 50% normal (that is, homozygous). You can just wait and hope to see if that proportion holds true in the nest, too. Besides, the question naturally pops up of how the heterozygous offspring can be picked out from among the homozygous ones when the natural coloration is dominant. (That means all the birds look alike because all carry the natural coloration genes, which mask the yellow genes in some of the birds.) There are ways to tell, but they take time.

In this case, I would first acquire a large stock of heterozygous breeding birds. Even yellow pied (or variegated) could show up, as reported in bird fancier literature (*AZ-Nachrichten*, *Agapornis* Breeder News, 11/

succeeding, and the young develop normally.

Yellow-green pied coloration has already made an appearance. In the Netherlands, purportedly pure (true breeding) intensely yellow Fischer's Lovebirds are available, which seems very appealing.

I believe that, at the moment, the creation of mutations is again well

experience, this species was one of my first acquisitions. So I can say without any reservation that a beginner can start just as well with Fischer's Lovebirds as with budgerigars or canaries, and not be headed for any disaster. I should comment, however, that these charming Africans don't particularly tolerate too well being transferred from a spacious

Photo by Vogelspark Walsrode

An imported flock of Fischer's Lovebirds, *Agapornis fischeri*.

73, Bochum, West Germany). It's said that yellow mated with yellow would produce a lethal factor, that is, the offspring would die as an embryo while still in the egg. The best possible mating is, accordingly, supposed to be heterozygous for yellow x yellow. For many years now, however, yellow x yellow crosses, too, have been

underway. We certainly expect some novelties, especially with Fischer's Lovebirds.

Fischer's Lovebird is an excellent aviary bird and reliable breeder. Many years ago, shortly before monetary reform, when I began to get interested in parakeets and parrots, and I had to start building up my own

aviary to a cramped indoor cage.

When Fischer's Lovebirds were one's first great love as a bird fancier, then this preference continues often enough for a lifetime. The noise is not unpleasant for most people's ears.

These small, so attractively colored Africans are charming, and one can't spend enough time marveling at their acrobatic antics. It's important to offer them a very varied diet, for they love variety to the point that they don't want to eat the same thing every day. Water-soluble vitamins in powder form are advisable as a winter supplement. The dosage is about 2 grams per pint of water (but see instructions in or on the package); remember that the bird drinks only about 6 or 7 ml of water a day, which means the individual dosage is a very small portion of the 2 grams.

Breeding success certainly doesn't depend upon how much expense the breeder can afford. The simplest breeding facilities suffice. Almost all of the recommendations made for Masked Lovebirds apply just as well to their close relatives, Fischer's Lovebirds.

One last, but important piece of advice, I believe, for breeders of colored birds is: never try for success in breeding mutations cheaply by starting with many birds despite their being too young or weak. All color varieties are less hardy and somewhat more susceptible to disease than normal birds, even though many sales-oriented breeders deny it.

Because of these reasons, it is highly probable that the young or underdeveloped color variety birds have only subnormal vitality and less than average life expectancy. And it's not uncommon for them to be deficient in expression of their coloration, too. That's not worth the breeder's investment.

In essence, even the new, completely inexperienced bird fancier can keep a pair of Fischer's Lovebirds, and, if he's bought from a reputable supplier, even hope to have some babies from them. The number of people interested in these birds has grown so much in the meantime that we now think of lovebirds as domestic animals. It's no longer difficult to mass-produce healthy, attractive youngsters from *Agapornis* species, especially that so-pleasingly-colored Fischer's Lovebird.

Photo by Michael Gilroy

A well-fed and well kept Fischer's Lovebird, *Agapornis fischeri.*

NYASA LOVEBIRD

AGAPORNIS PERSONATA LILIANAE

Agapornis lilianae has often been confused with *Agapornis roseicollis* (the Peach-faced or Rosy-faced Lovebird), and not just during the early days of discovery, either. You've got to take a close look. I have to admit that I've found other lovebirds more attractive, and that's why the Nyasa Lovebird only played guest roles in my aviary. Reports in earlier literature, which especially pointed out their alleged brooding mania, didn't inspire me to try my hand at breeding since I was also reading about the tendency of these birds to pluck their own young until they were naked and bloody in the nesting box. And that's precisely one of the few side effects in the breeding of ornamental birds which I, as an animal lover, find unpleasant. The scant availability of imported Nyasa Lovebirds certainly plays a role in the low level of their popularity among West German parrot fanciers. Malawi is today the center of the African source of lovebirds. The rather small, elongated biotope is not far from the range of the Black-cheeked Lovebird (*Agapornis personata nigriensis*). A certain focus of population density is supposed to have been observed in the Zambesi valley about 36 to 42 miles from Victoria Falls. Reliable information on any bans on the capture and export is not available at the moment.

Even though these birds have not become favorites, there are still bird fanciers who find this species to be the most charming, most affectionate to one another and the most good-natured and sociable of lovebirds. That is, real *love* birds. In fact, their gentleness towards other, unrelated species (cockatiels, budgerigars or forest birds) in the same enclosure is gratifying; I had to try it once myself because of the lack of space. There are exceptions, however, to their amiability towards one another.

Photo by Reinhard Tierfoto

The Nyasa Lovebird, Agapornis personata lilianae. This bird closely resembles the Peach-faced Lovebird, *Agapornis roseicollis.*

The Nyasa Lovebird was discovered in Northern Rhodesia in 1864. Their description as an independent species, however, is believed to have waited another three decades. The name *lilianae* refers to the reportedly very pretty sister of a renowned ornithologist of that time, Miss Lilian Sclater.

What was discovered there, was a small lovebird, that is, the smallest species with a white eye ring. A fully grown bird weighs 37 to 42 grams (1.3 to 1.5 ounces), with the female being the heavier of the two. Total length of this small, short-tailed parrot, from the tip of its tail is 13 to 14 cm (5 to 5.5 inches), according to Carl Aschenborn. A single outstretched wing measures a little over 8 cm (3 inches).

It's the sharper delineation of the red plumage, which, along with the differences in body size, that are supposed to avoid confusion with Peach-faced or Rosy-faced Lovebirds (*Agapornis p. roseicollis*), or with Fischer's Lovebirds (*Agapornis p. fischeri*). The reddish feathers of *Agapornis p. lilianae*—also different in shade of color— never go as far down on the neck or upper back. Eye ring, beak color and leg color are the same.

Differences in weight or plumage coloration don't help much in differentiating between the sexes. Hens are supposed to have duller red areas of the plumage, but I never noted that, and such minor differences are difficult to spot anyway.

One should be able to sex the young birds when they are seven to eight months old by observing their characteristic behavior in the flock. Young females begin to exhibit a mating stance—the stooped over or "ducking" sign of submission in the presence of males. The breeder should take this opportunity to mark the birds by clipping feathers or daubing with a harmless color.

The Nyasa Lovebird on display at the Vogelspark Walsrode who kindly supplied this photograph.

The British master breeder E.J. Boosey, on the other hand, wrote before the war (when he founded and then directed the Keston Foreign Bird Farm in Sussex) that the eye of the Nyasaland Lovebird should be examined during sunny weather or in bright illumination, when the eye color of fully adult males will look definitely darker.

Many of my readers will possibly appreciate these three tips which I certainly didn't want to omit, although I've never met any fellow German breeders who admitted to using them. According to expert advice from England, Nyasa Lovebirds should be at least 15 months old before being bred.

Thanks to their great adaptability, Nyasa Lovebirds, unlike many of their relatives, can be housed not only in aviaries, but also in boxes and flight cages. Imported birds are very timid at first and hide themselves for quite a while, even from their keeper. For those bred in captivity, however, the opposite is more often observed.

Similar differences apply to their vocalization; according to observations reported from Africa, the small flocks utter shrilly wide-ranging screams, with their startling and warning calls attaining a considerably high decibel level. If the same lovebirds become accustomed for several months to an enclosure, however, or if their offspring are bred in captivity, the noise is quite bearable in comparison with that of many other genera. The housing temperature for the Nyasa Lovebird should never fall below 50°F (10°C); for breeding, the temperature should be 62.6°F to 66.2°F (17°C to 19°C). According to my frequent experiences, unfortunately, the Nyasa Lovebird catches cold more readily than the other lovebirds.

As for feeding, a few peculiarities should be noted: *Agapornis* lovebirds are particularly fond of Japanese and Senegalese millet, whereas the familar millet spray, especially softened and slightly germinated, is popular as a treat. Finely chopped hardboiled (chicken) egg, as well as various rearing feeds for parakeets are well accepted, and it's always an advantage when the young get accustomed easily to a feed. Calcium and minerals can be well regulated by constant provision with pigeon grit. If you want to follow this advice starting right now, however, it's imperative that you start only with tiny amounts.

Fruits and greens are also important. These lovebirds are finicky and choosey, so you really can't help but try out many items anyway. Most of them decide upon chickweed, though they should keep right on getting dandelion because of its wholesome content and also because it protects against liver damage. They almost always enthusiastically nibble on peeled pieces of sweet apples. If you're accustomed to feeding your birds additional soft food then consider softened sweet raisin bread. For this purpose, honey water or sweet fruit juice is more appropriate than easily spoiled milk.

Vitamins or medicine drops are easy to add to food. Still green and milky (half-ripe condition) oats, wheat and corn are excellent supplemental food, and especially valuable during the breeding season. Branches and twigs for gnawing help to round out the menu, and are even supposed to prevent feather plucking among these birds.

It's been reported from the Zambesi valley that Nyasa Lovebirds like to eat from the ground, and to seek water spots for drinking and ample

An old drawing of a Nyasa Lovebird, *Agapornis lilianae*. These old drawings show the true colors and color patterns of the original wild birds imported from Africa.

bathing several times a day. In captivity, we certainly don't want to leave germinating food, fruit or greens on the ground, because they quickly become contaminated there.

The opportunity to bathe and have constant access to fresh drinking water are extremely important. I believe that the Nyasa Lovebird is sensitive to the quality of water. I found changes in my enclosure caused them to refuse the water. This was particularly pronounced in the difference between soft water and the highly chlorinated hard tap water of metropolitan Cologne. It can even lead to transient gastrointestinal disturbances; when the proportion of chemicals is very high in tap water, it should perhaps be reduced by boiling. Bath water should be fully boiled. Drinking water should be replenished with 50% fresh water to maintain a daily level.

According to Carl Aschenborn, the first Nyasa Lovebirds came to Germany in 1926. A year later, von Lucanus reported a hand-reared specimen which could even say a few words. Rudolf Neunzig successfully bred them the first year they were imported. At that time, it was reported in all seriousness that Nyasa Lovebirds essentially didn't have any other activity except reproduction. One had only to set up a small flock of this species in an aviary in order to have an abundant crop of offspring. Madame Lecallier, for example, in France, was ready to vouch for that. Aschenborn commented that they were the same as the other lovebird species. I, on the other hand, should by all rights be really convinced of it based upon old literature that the Nyasa Lovebird is downright obsessed with brooding. Although I still can't believe it, I'll cite E.J. Boosey just to finish this up: "If allowed, the

Nyasa Lovebird will breed without pause throughout the whole year, so that you'll constantly have either a clutch in the nest or young in the nesting box. I can't help but assume that this constant brooding is a behavioral quirk which adversely affects the health of both parents and offspring alike within a short time. However, it's no help to take the nesting boxes out of the free-flight enclosure, because then the Nyasa Lovebirds immediately succumb to colds in the winter if they have to spend a night in an aviary without being able to take refuge in a nesting box."

The question naturally arises as to why, under such favorable circumstances, such a super-fertile and problem-free reproducing parrot species is hardly seen anymore in the collections of bird fanciers. What was the reason? Why wasn't anything written on it? Despite years of importing thousands of them yearly, they apparently didn't attain any popularity as a pet. In the world of bird fanciers, such puzzling situations that remain so unexplained don't occur very often.

It's still quite difficult for me to accept the optimistic outlook of earlier days. Imported birds usually breed, surprisingly, more enthusiastically than those bred in captivity, which, in addition, would probably be more difficult to obtain.

Keeping them in an aviary is more promising as far as breeding success goes, and the colonial breeding system would perhaps also be good because it's natural. That would, in addition, also make

things easier because Nyasa Lovebirds are not considered pretentious in their selection of nesting sites nor in nesting material. Too bad, though, that colonial breeding is associated with a sizable risk: If at the time when all the baby lovebirds from different nests simultaneously become fledglings one of them

Photo by the San Diego Zoo

The question amongst bird lovers is why is this lovely sub-species, *Agapornis personata lilianae* so rarely available?

happens to beg for food from the wrong parents, vigorous biting can occur. Otherwise quite feasible reproduction in community enclosures, unfortunately, is associated not only with jealousy over food, but also with all the special rearing food being eaten up. And there's little that can be done about it.

The birds' wintering inside the house (perhaps even in boxes or flight cages) because of their sensitivity to cold if they were left outside, doesn't

lead to any problems of transition or loss in breeding drive. Good, invariably fertile breeding pairs actually brood several times successively all during the year without being affected to any great extent by weather changes or temperature fluctuations. The difficulty, however, is only to match up the right pair.

High-format nesting boxes especially suit Nyasa Lovebirds. The hen stuffs them full with a variegated array of different materials which she carries in her beak. The important items are large amounts of thin, flexible twigs, larger ones with bark that they'll scrape off, and long, half-wilted grass stalks. Likewise different from usual lovebird habits, the Nyasa Lovebirds pad the interior of their nests with grass stalks devoid of seedheads, eaten-up millet sprays and dry leaves— all of which should be provided for the birds. Coconut husk fibers, cut short, are a commercially available alternative. The floor of the nesting box is always packed inches deep, and, if there are enough building materials, the construction rises up on the sides and forms a dome or roof inside the nesting box.

Mention should be made again of the peculiarity of the cock, who, upon being introduced into the aviary, first busies himself with the nesting box, viewing it with obvious intensity, including a detailed interior inspection. I witnessed it three times during a temporary transfer into a large parakeet breeding unit which had just become available, so my observations are rather reliable since they were of different Nyasa Lovebirds each time.

A nest-selecting cock, so to speak, would be rather rare and a good indicator for differentiating the sexes and of readiness for breeding. I've never been able to confirm the alleged super-readiness to breed.

Clutches consist of three to seven eggs, some of which will be infertile, as a rule, representing somewhat a species-specific characteristic. The proportion of infertile eggs is not uncommonly 40–50%. The hen sits tight as soon as she's laid the first egg. The male brings food to her. The brood time is estimated at 20 to 23 days. The nestlings' first flights out of the nursery occur in 41 to 44 days. They have to be taken out sooner, however, for banding. One waits somewhat longer than with the more robust lovebirds, and, in my opinion, the 12th or 13th day is right, for Nyasa Lovebird nestlings are very frail.

If you build your own nesting boxes, unplaned and untreated boards 18 to 20 mm (0.7 to 0.8 inch) thick are needed. I recommend a square 17 x 17 cm (6.7 x 6.7 inches) surface area inside, and a 28 cm (11 inch) clearance above. The entrance hole is just right with a diameter of 48 mm (1.9 inches).

It's possible to bring the nesting box with the hatchlings still in it into the house when the autumn transfer is made (to avoid bad weather or dipping temperatures). The young lovebirds should be continued to be fed often enough. The attempt would certainly be worth the effort. If you leave the adult birds outside until the last possible moment, then you shouldn't try to

Photo by H. Reinhard Tierfoto

A wonderful pair of Nyasa Lovebirds, *Agapornis personata lilianae.*

prevent any renewed breeding fervor by taking away the nesting box which is precisely what will be needed as a refuge from the weather.

There are already supposed to be color mutations of the Nyasa Lovebird. The British artist, R.A. Vowles, who specializes in birds and has illustrated bird books, once painted a fine picture of a lutino (or buttercup yellow) which still retained the red on the head, a pleasing combination. The first lutinos or buttercup yellows appeared in 1935–1936, and in significant numbers by the mid-1950s. Parrot specialist Walter Lansberg, (Copenhagen, Denmark) has successfully bred the yellow variety. Dr. Burkard of Switzerland had so many of them that he could supply them to Germany.

Breeders in California probably obtained yellow breeding pairs from Australia and bred them, which is financially interesting. I have no knowledge of any German breeders doing so, although there certainly could be some who have. Nor have I seen any of these mutations myself. The first blue ones were recently reported in the U.S. Since the Nyasa Lovebird is also bred a great deal in South Africa, mutations can also be expected there. Crosses with Fischer's Lovebird are easily achieved. Fertile mixed breeds also occur with related species, as long as they have the white eye ring in common.

In summary the long-known Nyasa Lovebird, which was not very well known in Germany even in the years following the First World War, has up to today, and for unknown reasons, achieved only moderate popularity and distribution. Obtaining them is not quite so simple either; I found this out in 1980, although with some persistence is possible. Distribution and biotope in Africa, particularly in areas which are politically restless on a permanent basis, are comparatively small. There's complete uncertainty as to the size and chances of survival of present-day wild stocks. Specimens which escaped from South African breeding farms have been able to establish themselves in the wild. Recapture of Nyasa

Lovebirds is rather promising. These lovebirds even return voluntarily to their enclosure if their return is arranged correctly.

The Nyasa Lovebird is, I'm convinced, more sensitive and less resistant to weather than the more popular, larger lovebirds. I came across Danish reports that Nyasa Lovebirds could become infected with the human cold or grippe virus. This small parrot is an outsider without having deserved that condition. Although it's not clear which of its minor disadvantages is responsible for its relative unpopularity among parrot fanciers, the fact that it is unpopular, however, is regrettable. The African wild stocks could soon be in danger of extinction, and as it now stands, the species could hardly be kept permanently in aviaries. The Nyasa Lovebird receives very little attention, so I took particular effort to gain as much information on it as possible.

A lutino Nyasa Lovebird, *Agapornis p. lilianae.* The lutino is a color variety deficient in black color cells (melanophores).

Photo courtesy of the San Diego Zoo

with. The number of countries now breeding them has increased. South Africa and Australia are accomplishing a great deal, and the Japanese, with their special talent for coming up with new varieties, should be mentioned.

Peach-faced Lovebirds were the first lovebirds observed to carry nesting material around by tucking it into their own plumage. Their feathers are so constructed that their curved tips, with their particularly thick feather barbs or barbules firmly hold anything inserted into the plumage. If you watch the happy pair as they go about preparing their nursery, you're liable to doubt that the male really gets to help at all. At any rate, the female first bites into the pieces of nesting materials which were brought home, then chews them somewhat to soften them up. Only after that does the male have a chance to demonstrate his good will and possible talent as an architect or builder. The end result holds astonishingly well together. Peach-faced Lovebirds crunch up their nesting materials distinctly smaller than do their relatives from the same genus.

Despite their not so melodic song, if that's what you can even call this vocalization, these little parrots have meanwhile definitely attained the highest reaches of bird fancier's favor. They compensate for their shortcoming with a whole string of remarkable advantages, even if you still want to count their somewhat quarrelsome disposition as a negative aspect.

Peach-faced Lovebirds make first-class brooders, rearing up to three broods yearly, with hardly any concern for season or weather. The Peach-faced Lovebird is the leader in producing color varieties. Its

Photo by Reinhard Tierfoto

The yellow-green hybrid of the Peach-faced Lovebird, *Agapornis roseicollis*, is not a great talker. It is hardy, has three broods per year regardless of the season, and produces more color varieties than any other species of *Agapornis*.

domestication is already quite advanced, so breeders aren't too fastidious about diet, etc.

Somewhat hesitatingly, I'm going to meet my obligation of telling you that the din these small, colorful Africans produce can make keeping them in closely built residential areas a problem. It's mainly the screeching chorus which is unpleasant, and which, for usually inexplicable reasons, can resound in the aviary for half a minute, or even for a whole minute. During that short time, many a sensitive person wants to hold his hands over his ears. The mutual contact call sounds like *uek-uek*, and is normally given twice. The warning signal given when frightened sounds about the same, but is uttered 15 to 25 times in rapid succession. A squeak or squeal, for example, is their reaction to the sudden appearance of a cat in the enclosure. When violent fighting breaks out among them, all possible kinds of screaming, screeching and shrieking fill the air, similar to a budgerigar uproar. I think it's important to look a little more closely for a moment at these quarrels which often break out among the birds.

We shouldn't overly condemn this innate predisposition, which, in my opinion, people do all too often. According to my numerous experiences, some unusual event or imagined threat leads to the hysterical behavior in the Peach-faced Lovebird, and it's especially the males which are given to really going berserk. It assumes the proportions of contagious emotional upheaval leading to general screaming, followed by tumultuous fighting to the point that feathers fly. I've repeatedly had to intervene with the garden hose when the opportunity presented itself—it's always effective, but should be used only in warm summer weather.

If these private wars continue, then it may become

necessary to clear out the aviary and redistribute the birds, assigning them to several different enclosures to avoid fatalities. On the other hand, breeders have been urged for decades, for heaven's sake, not to keep two Peach-faced Lovebird pairs in the same brooding compartment. Today, however, colonial breeding—the normal situation in Africa—is practiced often and successfully in flight cages. When I, however, tried it as early as the mid-1950s, everyone who heard about it was horrified at such an absurdity, and there was no lack of dire warnings. Yet, I was encouraged by the man who sold me my first breeding pairs of Peach-faced Lovebirds, and who kept a very large flock in a massive garage where he let them mate and brood at will. There I saw with my own eyes the kind of squabbles mentioned earlier, which sometimes seemed quite dangerous, but apparently never led to any serious injury. The breeder, too, confirmed that. So I provided ample space in the aviary (about 197 x 71 x 79 inches), and am convinced that this is a good prerequisite. However—and I'd like to impress this upon my readers—only guaranteed pairs should be placed at the same time and on the same late afternoon in an enclosure provided with at least double the number of similar nesting boxes. Excess females or males would guarantee prompt fighting. It follows logically, therefore, that in case of death, the dead bird be replaced immediately, or else the surviving mate be removed.

I recommend three pairs of lovebirds for a small-scale colonial breeding set-up. That way, according to my own attempts, harmony is easiest to achieve and maintain. Although I've often seen far more pairs put together for breeding, even five pairs seem to be risky, and any more than that seems sheer frivolity; it might succeed,

Photo by Glen Scott Axelrod

Keeping colonies of lovebirds is fine if you can stand the noisy uproars which occur from time to time. But Peach-faced Lovebirds have been known to be aggressive against weaker birds, often killing or maiming them.

however, if the space were very large. On the other hand, anyone with some talent at building things could enable three to five pairs to keep visual contact yet be separated from one another. That's the second proven practical tip that I would like to give here. Naturally, the feeling of togetherness engenders breeding fervor, if

you avoid quarreling.

Regular observation of lovebird enclosures is always recommended, and, if you're in luck, you'll be made aware in time by the noisy uproar. If fighting breaks out among the females over certain nesting boxes, then resolutely remove the bone of contention.

Our beautiful Peach-faced Lovebirds will definitely maim or kill weaker birds when they feel like it, above all during the breeding preparations. Our large lovebirds are not too suitable for a community aviary unless it's on a bird farm. The predominant method of lining up outside flights makes it advisable to make double walls of wire mesh screening in such a way that hollow or dead space is created by sandwiching the structural posts between the two wire screens. Without this precaution, a few nestlings in the adjoining sections will soon lose a leg.

It's too bad that one can hardly speak of courtship behavior in the case of Peach-faced Lovebirds. Perhaps you can observe the way that many hens beg food from their choice of a cock by swaying their heads. Others assume a posture with the neck tilted to one side, as if they were embarrassed or ashamed, when they want the male to mount for mating. The mating drive in this species is very pronounced, defending their nests to the point of self-sacrifice, whereby their dangerously sharp, stout beaks are by nature excellent weapons. At times like these, even larger parakeets such as rosellas or cockatiels get their share of bites. If you intend to try breeding, consider that at times young birds are ready to breed at four to five months of age. Whenever that occurred, however, despite the precautions I took, results were rarely satisfactory. Hens so young are very subject to egg-binding, and not uncommonly succumb to it. In their own interest, it can be recommended that breeders breed only birds which are at least one year old, when gratifying breeding results may be achieved. You can certainly feel comfortable about waiting that long, because lovebirds remain fertile for many years. German breeding lines breed readily throughout almost the whole year; this holds true, however, only in aviaries.

Despite whatever may have been written about the subject, I've found again and again that the pretty little creatures lose a lot of their breeding fervor when they are kept in cages or in banks of breeding units. I once had to keep six breeding pairs for a whole winter, from November to April, in flight cages in my home because rats had gained access to my garden set-up. One couldn't any longer fail to see that such confined living conditions lead to premature loss of spirit or liveliness and to dulling of the senses. The birds began to really grieve and in no case would have been disposed to breed. Even the interest in each other of firmly joined couples decreased from week to week. That's a serious handicap to breeding, yet the male always remained near his mate and brought food for her into the cage from time to time.

Because Peach-faced Lovebirds are the most kept and most bred lovebirds, it is hardly any wonder that many keepers feel called to give advice. Many fanciers of this species have perhaps already had to suffer for it, because there were recommendations, for example like: "Nesting boxes must absolutely be hung in the open, uncovered part of the aviary, where they can be fully exposed to all showers and rainfall. In the event of a summer dry spell, the keeper should intensively humidify nesting facilities

hygrometers, but for my taste, avicultural enclosures and cleverly designed air-conditioned production facilities are two different things. Whoever can and wants to afford such sophistication, make note of my experience with the owner of a super set-up like that. What a large automatic moisturizer and ventilation system really does excellently is to spread and uniformly distribute bacteria and other pathogenic organisms. The

Photo by Dr. Herbert R. Axelrod

A lovely Peach-faced Lovebird which Dr. Axelrod maintains in old aquariums with large perches inside the tank. This keeps the dust from food and feathers from flying around the house, but cages are much better accomodations for lovebirds.

with the garden hose, etc." I don't like to speak harshly, but such advice seems stupid to me! As an old hand at this business, I was just as unable to comply with the advice not to allow the atmospheric humidity in the breeding area to drop below 65% under any circumstances. Do you know, perhaps, how to regulate that in a normal outside aviary? There are, of course, hygrometers, and even atmospheric humidifiers automatically controlled by

result of breeding birds in that way was that six subsequent years of proper control and expenses could not re-establish a healthy situation.

When I first started, I, too, went along with humidification procedures, and was rewarded with failures. It's true that the crucial aspects of our Peach-faced Lovebirds in Africa are often associated with flight distances to rivers or lakes, yet there are also long dry plumage colors of the maturing bird can be more or less recognized, it soon attempts to leave the nest. I found the average time in the nest was 37 days. Isolated instances of 32 or even 43 days occurred. All the young of one brood don't necessarily leave their nesting box on the same day.

If the hen should already begin laying the next clutch even before the first nestlings are independent, it's a good idea to hang another wooden nesting box of the same kind right next to it. The evening will come, most probably, when the mother will no longer tolerate her first brood.

The last moment to separate older from younger birds is when the younger birds begin to show sexual maturity. A flight section is the best arrangement for encouraging the young birds to exercise. Don't forget to hang up the same kind of nesting boxes, which will still be needed for a while as refuge and perhaps also as a sleeping niche. The young can still look smaller and thinner than their parents, yet weigh as much.

Opinions on the age at which the young become independent differ astonishingly. I've repeatedly experienced how it depends upon the number of nestmates, nutrition, weather and season. The earliest I've witnessed was about nine weeks after hatching, and the longest was almost four months. Another problem that needs to be resolved is in reference to the squabbles that break out when pairs form later in the aviary holding these younger birds.

The reader will have already noted that, as a future breed of Peach-faced Lovebirds, he won't get far with just a single-compartment aviary. The more space and compartments available, the better the chances of chick growth and development. Although German (and other northerly) breeding lines are always hardier, wintering in the open is risky! Indoor enclosures (without nesting boxes) in which both sexes can build up their strength for the coming breeding season are the better alternative, for cool drafts are a significant health hazard. Nesting boxes can be left as sleeping quarters only where male and female are separated; otherwise, breeding attempts will be made, which could lead to the female's death due to egg-binding or to death of any hatchlings born in the cold. If, however, the whole flock molts in late autumn, then the mating fervor is quenched for months, which saves the breeder having to take many precautions.

No long lists of recommendations need be written any more on feeding *Agapornis roseicollis*. Special packaged feeds are on the market; these powerful birds can easily handle large, hard seeds. A level teaspoon of hemp seed for each bird daily suffices in warm weather, but this amount can be doubled when the birds have become fledglings, or when cool autumn and cold winter set in. If the young are still being fed by their parents, it's demonstrably better to give some wheat and niger seed,

Lifting the covers off the nest box, you get a glimpse of three Peach-faced Lovebird squeakers about 16 days old.

Photo by Louise Van der Meid

which are also nutritious and supplement one another. Linseed and buckwheat can be used from time to time for variety.

Every Peach-faced Lovebird which learns to like apples, pears and other garden fruit, and which eventually nibbles every green leaf, not uncommonly develops an obviously smooth and especially brilliant plumage. And that's all the more unfortunate, because it's difficult to bring the best out of other, more finicky birds of the same genus, because they have only a moderate taste for those supplemental foods. The most promising thing to do is to start by giving thin, fresh twigs, which they should be getting to know as nesting materials anyway.

I'm often asked what rearing food I recommend as soon as the young become audible in the nesting boxes. I don't consider it absolutely necessary, but I do resort to certain supplemental feeding if more growth substances seem advisable. Besides the well-known egg food every other day, I also occasionally give some packaged parakeet feed and a tablespoon of prepared soft feed or mash.

It was not unusual to read that too much oil-rich seed causes self-plucking and feather loss, plucking of the young or even stroke. I've never experienced any relationships like that, and I also do not advocate completely depriving the birds of hemp seed. This seed contains, besides the oil, other stimulative substances that have beneficial effects that have been long since recognized.

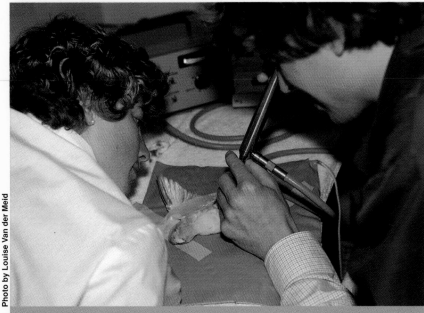

Photo by Louise Van der Meid

Veterinarians are able to anesthetize lovebirds and, with a special device, look at the birds' reproductive organs to ascertain its sex.

COLOR VARIETIES OR COLOR MUTATIONS

This subject seduces avicultural writers into coming up with concepts and formulas which mean very little to the majority of readers. Happily, you don't have to be an expert in these things if you want to deal with professional breeders. It's enough to have a breeding objective, and to apply helpful printed guidelines to forecast the results which given matings can be expected to produce. Not uncommonly, however, these guidelines are not fully understood, so we have a new victim who spreads the word that "color breeding is something which only scientists can properly grasp." I've met with such grossly exaggerated views often enough.

The first color mutations in Peach-faced Lovebirds were achieved (or at least first observed) during the Second World War. The lutino or buttercup was an early one; it's sex linked and produces an intensely yellow bird that still retains the red part of its plumage. Normal yellow (more frequently and poetically called *golden cherry*) appeared in the mid-1950s in Japan. Europe's first shipment was imported by Burkard into Switzerland; his first published report (in *Feathered Friends*, an official publication of the Swiss aviculturists) was a sensation. About 1962, yellow-green pied (or harlequin) birds with quite uniquely contrasted areas of plumage appeared in California. The effect of piebaldness, however, varies in every bird. A breeding ideal would be 50% pied with as uniform a distribution of color as possible. The pink or reddish mask remains unchanged. The pied is an attractive variant.

The blue mutation—so to say the crowning glory of color mutations among the

Possibly, too, the newly banded birds won't live long, for in their understandable efforts to throw out the foreign body, parents naturally throw out their own young from the nesting box with it. The fall is either immediately fatal, depending upon the height, or later due to cold weather. It's advisable to attach the band to Peach-faced Lovebirds on the fifth or sixth day after hatching. Supervision must be guaranteed over the following 14 days, and once this time is over, the parents will, to some extent, have gotten used to the new situation. It might be a good idea to dip the shiny bands into diluted non-toxic black lacquer. Personally, I

never had any problem with closed banding. A suitable system I use for temporarily recording age, brood, sex, etc., consists of cutting clearly visible long feathers or of marking with daubs of non-toxic color, plus, of course, the appropriate noting of it in my record book.

I'm still enthralled by Peach-faced Lovebirds, and my varied experience with precisely this species has been incorporated in this book. These, perhaps most attractive representatives of the lovebirds, gave me my first great success in parrot breeding, so something like that remains as a memorable impression in the life of a

hobbyist. Aren't these colorful little Africans exquisite creatures? And they're also easy to keep, simple to feed, and are increasingly becoming favorites of hobbyist breeders. The beautiful color varieties, especially, are attracting more and more enthusiastic fans.

The literature on lovebirds is finally improving in specialized German publications after decades of undeserved stagnation. I believe that the great and continuing interest in this bird family can really use some support in the literature. And it's precisely with our Peach-faced Lovebirds that this support is clearly evident.

Photo by Horst Mueller

A compatible group of Peach-faced Lovebirds, *Agapornis roseicollis* in normal coloration.

Some color varieties of the Peach-faced Lovebird. The common names given to many color varieties varies according to the breeder.

This magnificent photograph shows the variation in the colors of the feathers of a Peach-faced Lovebird in flight. Note that it's feet are not tucked in the way many long-distance flying birds are.

A cobalt lovebird and a pastel blue lovebird. That's the names of the color varieties as known in Scotland where the photographer, Michael Gilroy, resides.

BLACK-WINGED LOVEBIRD

AGAPORNIS TARANTA

Also known as the Abyssinian Lovebird, *Agapornis taranta*, likewise a large lovebird, has increased in popularity, although imports now as much as ever are few and certainly lag behind the demand for them. As far as I know, imports have been almost at a full standstill since 1979. The supply of domestically bred birds improved, although in many areas today it takes a little looking around to find some.

Male Black-winged Lovebirds attain about 17 to 18 cm (6.7 to 7 inches) total body length and weigh, as I've often determined from dead males, 45 to 48 grams (1.6 to 1.7 ounces). This weight in proportion to size shows that this species has a tendency to become overweight. Since pictures usually depict males, we can say that the ground color of the female is the same as that of the male, except that she lacks the red on the head. Breeders are happy and relieved that the sexes can be so easily told apart because this makes it easier to pair up real breeding mates (often one of the greatest problems in starting to breed other lovebirds in this genus).

At first, young birds look like females, even though in the early stages the beak is still yellowish brown. Young Black-winged males stand out once the first dark red little feathers sprout out of the forehead or around the eyes, thus making differentiation easy for the breeder. It's just a myth, in my opinion, that experts can see the difference while the young are still in the nest, and I don't think it would be reasonable to start inspecting nests just for that reason. According to my own observations, you've got to wait about a hundred days before you can see the male's red feathers without handling the bird. If, however, you insist on doing that, despite the fact that the lovebirds emphatically dislike being handled, then it's certainly possible to poke around and separate the head plumage with a matchstick or something to look for the red earlier. Complete coloration takes about 270 to 280 days. During that time, a first molt can occur, which, however, depends upon birth date and season.

Imported birds remain reserved and distrustful for quite some time, which is why they acclimate so slowly under new conditions. On the other hand, captive-bred Black-winged Lovebirds are often tamer than many of their closest relatives. Their

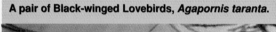
A pair of Black-winged Lovebirds, *Agapornis taranta.*

Photo by Reinhard Tierfoto

Drawing by Eric Peake

The Black-winged Lovebird, *Agapornis taranta*, is also known as the Abyssinian Lovebird. This drawing shows a male (with the red forehead) and a female without a marked forehead.

vocalizations even in a small flock are hardly unpleasant at all. Occasionally you might hear a short, loud screech. Their chirps and twitterings are frequently almost melodious. Black-winged Lovebirds are perhaps ideal for room aviaries, that is, where walls are thin and neighbors plentiful. You can only appreciate that once you've heard the loud piercingly shrill cries of other parrots.

On the other hand, they are somewhat quarrelsome. Bickering and squabbles are common particularly near their nesting sites, which also function as a refuge. The female usually takes the initiative in skirmishes and perseveres the longest. I'm convinced that with *Agapornis taranta*, the male is the "weaker sex." Those who imported large numbers of this lovebird and dealt with them and kept them in flights know that the mortality rate of males is considerably higher than that of females. It was always that way in imported shipments, in which dead males predominated in the shipping containers. Today, although only the well-initiated know it, imported males die chiefly during acclimatization, quarantine, and changeover in diet.

Neither sex likes to be handled and both are prone to injury when caught in nests. I had the feeling that although in my aviary this particular lovebird species passionately bathed in fresh, flowing water, this passion doesn't really fit in with their decidedly arid native mountain highlands. I question the limitation of their distribution to sparsely vegetated mountain ranges devoid of human contact, as reported in the older literature on parrots. Years of acquaintance with a jet airline pilot on the Addis Ababa-to-Capetown route convinced me that the far from shy Black-winged Lovebirds flew around quite confidently in gardens on the outskirts of Addis Ababa. My friend was able to photograph them from his hotel balcony.

Another fact which I clearly perceived during many years of keeping birds is just as interesting in itself as meaningful in care, maintenance and breeding: Black-winged Lovebirds are surprisingly quick to try foods they don't know yet. So you can get them used to supplemental foods.With their readiness to try strange food, they stand at the head of all other lovebirds.

These little parrots, moreover, are astonishingly alert. Relatives of mine who were sleeping on the grounds not far from the bird enclosure told me they heard a loud hue and cry, and shrill screaming every night about midnight. As I kept watch to see what was happening one night, it turned out that a rat had penetrated the anteroom of the shelter and was eating grain stored there. The many other birds in the aviary didn't make a peep and hardly stirred. The adult cockatiels hissed, but that doesn't carry far. Only the small Africans gave the alarm!

I've got to praise the Black-winged Lovebird's robustness and winter hardiness, that is, as long as it's noted that very cold winters seldom hit the Cologne bight. So perhaps hobbyists in colder places shouldn't take a chance, but it's certain that these proud birds are clearly hardier than all of their lowland relatives from hot steppes and jungles.

You can call their behavior rather charming, as long as they're well acclimated or else born and reared in the hobbyist's aviary. At times other than during the breeding season, they are even rather friendly as a group. Only the uninitiated fanciers doubt that, for it goes without saying that there are indeed some monthly fighting bouts, threats, hue and crying bloody murder, and hacking, all of which, however, lead to injuries only in exceptional cases. If you know that right from the start, you'll worry less. Moreover, all the quarrelsomeness at the feeding stations observed with many parrots is, surprisingly, hardly seen with Black-winged Lovebirds.

In large flight enclosures you can observe what is probably close to the norm in the wild, namely, adherence to a form of daily routine. Males tend to stay out of squabbles started and carried out by the females. If they insist on getting involved, however, they do it vocally, but rarely more actively than that. The reason may be perhaps that the males have long known what the breeder is just finding out: the ladies of this *Agapornis* species bite considerably more painfully and piercingly. After a successful squabble, they are fed and finally tenderly caressed as a reward by their mate. These insights are the fruits of long observation.

I've never seen them perform a typical courtship ritual, somewhat like males carrying out particular movements. Or should we consider their hopping from one side to the other of the females (which amuses children) as a sort of wooing? The male attends with great interest the close-up first inspection of the selected nesting box, twittering quite excitedly, hopping to and fro, and visibly enraptured. The female, who finally reappears, is ceremoniously rewarded with food from his crop. There is also just as good a chance that the female, reappearing after her inspection of the nesting box, begs for the reward, so to speak, by distinctly nodding her head. All of this is extremely interesting and moving for the quiet observer.

The brooding fervor of the female, as I've often observed, can also be expressed by her carrying, in her plumage, items which are actually unsuitable for nest-building. It's often possible to carry out a test by using paper scraps, which is perhaps not always reliable, but is indeed a nice little experiment. I've never seen males fully slip into a nesting box chosen by their females. They're satisfied with peeking through the entrance hole, peering down from the roof or over from the perch. During this time they become somewhat more aggressive towards curious onlookers of either their own or other species in the aviary if they come too close to the future nursery. If, during a moment of inattention, another female slips into the nesting box, it's only the female who rightly belongs there who throws the intruder right out, as if this were an agreed upon division of labor.

The formation of mating pairs among Black-winged Lovebirds, which are not flocking birds, proceeds harmoniously and steadfastly. Scratching of heads seems to be a definite need, so much so that tame birds let the hobbyist spoil them like that, scratching their heads. Those who want to experiment or save space by setting up a community aviary (although it's not really advisable) should provide ample escape room or structures, and introduce only larger feathered companions who know how to defend themselves. The sensitive legs of the companions are always somewhat at risk, though. Cockatiels are indeed larger than lovebirds, but don't defend themselves as well when the chips are down. At first, the cockatiel probably has to take a few lumps and can only be considered good social company if he isn't injured seriously.

Ample nesting sites in as many different forms and sizes as possible should be readied by breeders when several pairs are kept together. The ones which are not used can be removed later if doing so doesn't create any disturbance. The choice of large nesting boxes avoids brood-inhibiting bones of contention from the very start. Excess boxes serve as refuge and sleeping areas. Following successful or even aborted brooding, I've always removed the padding and nesting materials because they attract vermin, but left the boxes, considering their possible additional functions. If an exception to this rule is in order, then several years of

experience and instinct will guide the breeder. In this context I'd also like to emphasize that my successful breeding pairs never made second attempts to brood during the same year. Unfortunately, observations in the wild are scant, so we don't know whether, at least in Ethiopia, two broods occur in close succession, which would be possible climatically.

Nest construction is so divergently carried out that I thoroughly understand why descriptions vary so considerably. As I already wrote in 1976, Black-winged Lovebirds are rather negligent in their interior decoration and don't build any roofing dome. Not uncommonly, only a very thin layer is laid down on the floor of the nesting box. In their almost vegetation-free homeland, building materials are scarce.

It's certain, too, that there are even pairs which only somewhat symbolically build a nest. The female of one of my own long-fruitful pairs carried very little inside the nesting box. I placed the nesting box in such a way that I could help, for even the materials which finally got inside were poorly utilized. I don't want to bring up my many years of breeding success, since I took the simplest way, which consisted of buying an already proven pair. Indeed, I even took the pair's familiar nesting box right along with me and hung it up in their new home in about the same spot as it hung in the old one. Perhaps it should be mentioned that it was small inside and almost too cramped for any numerous batch of nestlings. There were, however, never more than three fledglings inside. Could that have been because of insufficient space? Not much padding material would have fit inside, but thank heaven that only finches have the urge to pack and stuff to the rim.

One of the breeding females who once had lived in an aviary near a chicken farm preferred chicken feathers for padding the nest, but never tried to bite them into smaller pieces. I offered her long wilted grass, empty millet stalks and peeled bark strips. Only a few fragments were taken inside; I tossed a handful inside, thinking of the moisture reserve in it.

The aviary brooding season lasts from the end of February to October, inclusively, an unusually long season. Depending upon what season the brooding occurs, hatching takes place after 24 to 29 days. Alert readers will see at once that it's faster with the lowland species of our beautiful lovebirds. All things being equal the development of the young takes an average of 46 days or often longer to the first time they leave the nest; then the young go in and out for a few more days. Based upon many years of experience, though only with the same breeding pairs, but supplemented by exchange of information with my colleagues, I assume that a lot of lack of success is because the nesting accommodations are not acceptable to the birds. They may have been made too large, though with good intentions, or perhaps offered more floor area than overhead clearance, and were not replaced despite unequivocal rejection; it has

never been of much use to try to force birds in any way.

It just so happens that I can support this by my own observations: when an old nesting box (brought from the aviary near the chicken farm mentioned above) became shabby—such items, naturally, mustn't be chemically impregnated—I gave my proven breeding Black-winged lovebirds a tree-stump hollow, thinking I had provided them with something 100% natural. The birds, however, didn't share my opinion for a moment, and went out on a brood strike for the year . . . the female letting her eggs fall from the perch to the ground. Judging from her behavior, I'd almost like to assume that right from the start, she didn't like the dimensions of the task of building her new nest. Nesting materials were piled up on the top cover, but hardly anything was carried into the hollow. I had to slap together a facsimile of the old nesting box.

The usual clutch is three to six eggs, and one egg is laid more or less every day until the goal is reached. Once the hen finally settles down on the nest, her mate shows himself to be an exemplary provider. Later, both parents take turns feeding the young. The young apparently grow much too slowly at first, if you compare them with the perennially popular budgerigar. At first, even the head looks larger than the rest of the body, and the horrified breeder suspects malformation. Even by day six the little birds are so tiny that the breeder assumes the worst and wants to resort to hand-feeding. Yet, such an attempt

at such an early stage would hardly have any chance of succeeding.

A breeder of Black-winged Lovebirds must remind himself every year that the eggs are indeed laid at intervals, and it follows, therefore, that the tiny nestlings will show great differences. Even if it seems like it, they are usually neither neglected or half-starved, nor retarded, and will ordinarily recover. After 11 to 14 days, their eyes open. In about two weeks, the first pin-feathers appear on the rear part of the body, and some longer ones come through the skin on the wings. At an age of about 35 days, the plumage of the young bird is more or less formed. An initial molt is not the norm, but is possible at an age of four to five months.

The male parent has the task of feeding the fledgling Black-winged Lovebirds for awhile in the cage or enclosure. This fading can go on to the end of the 11th week of life, whereby the quantity is progressively reduced as the young learn to feed themselves. At the start of the 12th week I removed the young birds (more out of habit than actual necessity) from the part of the aviary where they had been living with their parents. They were housed in an adjacent enclosure where visual and audible contact remained often enough through the separating wall of single-ply wire screening. My experiences showed that these lovebirds are good parents.

Black-winged Lovebirds seem not to mind being moved around, and grown birds easily and rapidly adapt to new conditions and surroundings. I've never witnessed aggression towards the young birds. The father indeed continued often enough to feed his begging sons and daughters long after the usual period of parental care was over. Young females often get the most because they know how to beg more intensively.

only very rarely mate twice in the same year. So far as I've been able to follow up individual reports, the events occurred in indoor aviaries or breeding units. The alleged persecution can certainly result from cramped space, which makes even the gentlest of creatures aggressive.

remain within territorial limits. Therefore, each pair also defends a small territory of only a few square yards around its nesting hollow, and doesn't simply fly away when disturbed, as do many other birds.

A recent detailed breeding report (written in German by Lietzoff in the 8/1980

Photo by Dr. Herbert R. Axelrod

A chick Black-winged Lovebird almost fully feathered.

Of course, I've heard and read the opposite, for example, of attacks upon the young ready for their first mating season, by the older birds who are going through another period of mating fervor. Frankly, I often doubt such allegations, for, as I've already mentioned, lovebirds

Successful free-flying experiments with Black-winged Lovebirds in various countries support the observation that their territorial sense is very pronounced, which corresponds again to the African mode of life, where even the smallest groups

Lovebird Breeders' Bulletin, *AZ-Nachrichten*) states that the interval between the laying of eggs can also be longer than 24 hours. He fed the pair mainly germinated sunflower seed and hemp seed as well as grated carrots as soon as definite incubation began. Note that he bred in a large flight cage in a centrally heated room. The nesting site was hung outside the cage. Humidifiers (water containers) were hung on radiators in the room to maintain humidity. In addition, Lietzoff sprayed a little water daily around the breeding room. For all of that, the first brood was a problem I've never had. Under some circumstances that could be ascribed to the heating, which indeed even kills wood worms! In aviaries, embryo death hardly occurs, at least in Abyssinian lovebirds.

Lietzoff's second attempt was successful. The eggs hatched 24, 25 and 26 days after laying. The hatchlings looked rather naked for a few days, though they were covered with thin, gray down. At the age of 14 days, the green appeared on the wing coverts. You've often got to wait somewhat longer, however, according to my own observations. Lietzoff's statement that his grown Abyssinians were left until 17 weeks old in the same cage with their parents seems very vurious to me. Also, he states that all slipped back into the nesting box at night. The parents finally lost patience after four and a half months. No probable cause can be assumed for surprising change in behavior, since the pair most likely didn't have in mind trying any second mating. The breeding food described above also included a prepared parakeet feed, along with dandelion leaves to provide vitamins, and abundant pieces of apple.

The most impressive part of this exemplarily presented breeding report seems to me to be the successful snapshots of 15-day-old nestlings, as well as young Black-winged Lovebirds 11 weeks old.

I have not yet heard anything reliable about color varieties in Black-winged Lovebirds, either mutations or changes achieved by breeders. And that doesn't mean, of course, that something like that can't occur in the meantime or one day in the future! Crosses with Black-masked and Fischer's Lovebirds are said to have succeeded in isolated cases.

Especially since Black-winged Lovebirds hardly differ from other lovebirds in nutrition, I'd like to say something based upon my own studies, and which I've previously published: Black-winged Lovebirds can tolerate a much greater proportion of fat-rich seeds in their feed than would be allowable for their obesity-prone relatives. They prefer larger seeds such as oats, hemp, white sunflower, and like to take wild berries and fruit from the forest as supplementary food.

We can assume that because of the continual political and belligerent events in the birds' African homeland, only sporadic imports of these birds will be forthcoming. Keep in mind that this species was discovered and described as long ago as 1814, yet despite that it took nine decades before the first imports. Moreover, there's talk of a subspecies, *Agapornis* ta*ranta nana*, which is supposed to have shorter wings and beak. Despite my getting around quite a bit and knowing European importers well, I've never yet seen this subspecies.

Viewed from my ivory tower, I would welcome it if hobbyist groups would promote more breeding of Black-winged Lovebirds and encourage it with prizes. Judges should have ample opportunity to acquire knowledge in the proper judging of this species of lovebird.

In the interest of all lovebirds and their breeders, properly held shows and exhibitions are of considerable importance for dealing with the results of breeding for performance and specific races or breeds.

Participation at such events, however, involves effort, risks and expenses. And one cannot expect many to show up with their home-bred lovebirds as long as they cannot be assured that their achievements will be evaluated properly by knowledgeable experts. That describes rather precisely my own deliberations and decision to avoid taking my lovebirds on the road to shows. I didn't believe that the benefits outweighed the expense and risks of yanking my birds out of their comfortable enclosure. Winter exhibits also involve problems of change in temperature and cold. In 1982, however, the classes were expanded, though much has yet to be learned.

Bird fanciers still often consider the Black-winged Lovebird to be the most fastidious and difficult species to breed. I, personally, haven't had that experience, that is, as long as I offered variously constructed and, above all, differently sized wooden nesting boxes for the birds to select. Not uncommonly, the breeding pair selects the smallest model. Their homeland territory is often covered by cold, humid fog, and the weather is clouded over and rainy, with nighttime temperatures under the freezing point. During the day, after clearing up and some sunshine for awhile, the temperature rises to 82.4°F. Birds which endure this kind of climate have a robust constitution; however, as already noted, the males become sick more easily than do the females.

Photo by H.Reinhard Tierfoto

This wonderful photograph shows the Black-winged Lovebird, *Agapornis taranta*, in flight.

RED-FACED LOVEBIRD

AGAPORNIS PULLARIA

It's rather surprising that just one lovebird species has such completely different nesting habits from the other, yet very closely related, lovebirds. But that's not the only peculiarity.

Known also as the Red-headed Lovebird, *Agapornis pullaria* possesses the most extensive range of distribution of all members of the genus; it extends approximately across the middle of the African continent like a broad continous ribbon. This enormous biotope cuts variously through the geography and fauna of the sovereign territories of numerous African nations. So it's all the more surprising that, despite the extensive distribution, only very little is known of the Red-faced Lovebird in the wild; to make it even more surprising, flocks of them are in the habit of foraging for miles about. In the evening they all return to familiar trees for roosting, at which point the tropical night falls and any further observation becomes difficult. Their shyness keeps the observer at bay even in the early morning, when as a rule their tall, isolated roosting trees can hardly be approached without alerting them. They spend the day in little groups of six to nine birds.

Red-faced Lovebird populations are found from the Gold Coast and Sierra Leone through Cameroon to Northern Angola, as well as in large areas of the Congo basin, Lake Albert and Lake Kivu. In addition, they also extend from the Sudan to Northern Tanzania. According to reports from the region around in the city of Entebbe, experts verify the presence of a subspecies in Uganda. In view of this immense distribution, we can happily consider any danger of extinction to be improbable for a long time yet to come.

In early 17th-century England, it was precisely the Red-faced Lovebird who had already come to be a domestic favorite of elegant noble ladies, a fact which astonishes us today. Birds imported earlier always had clipped wings, so they didn't look as nice and arrived in very poor health. Mortality was clearly and discouragingly high, yet the survivors enjoyed the best chances of continuing to survive and to endure in the well-heated salons of the

The Red-faced Lovebird, *Agapornis pullaria*, is sometimes called the Red-headed Lovebird. It is the most widely distributed of all lovebirds and is found throughout central Africa.

Photo by Wolfgang de Grahl

well-to-do. Keeping imported birds outside in enclosures the same year they arrive is not advisable even today. Wintering inside the house is preferable as a rule.

And yet it may be worthwhile for the lovebird enthusiast to take advantage of any Red-faced Lovebirds offered for sale. It's currently believed that they are less suitable for keeping in a cage than are their more saleable relatives; cramped housing easily causes them to suffer melancholy, which can express itself by the otherwise quite active little parrot sitting passively around, or even by their mutually plucking out each other's feathers. Moreover, in cages, the tail feathers are damaged so much that they look shabby. In aviaries, the birds like to gnaw any accessible wooden parts of the construction. Smaller cage-mates such as, for example, finches or canaries, have to tolerate all sorts of annoyances, and nests of ornamental birds of lower position in the social hierarchy are not uncommonly wantonly destroyed by Red-faced Lovebirds.

Every open aviary should have a refuge, since, in contrast to the majority of lovebirds, Red-faced ones don't particularly like wooden nesting boxes as overnight accommodations, and there's a sensitivity towards drafts.

All told, we have a negative picture, if you compare Red-faced Lovebirds with their more popular relatives. On the other hand, a small flock of Red-faced Lovebirds makes a decidedly pretty sight. Their frequently uttered call is

An old drawing by Eric Peake shows the color of the original Red-faced Lovebird.

never unpleasantly loud, and hardly upsets the neighbors. Tolerance towards equally large or somewhat larger bird species is on the whole rather good—which is a fact that at first I scarcely wanted to believe until I was forced to introduce a few male Red-faced Lovebirds into a showcase aviary of a pet shop I managed for many years.

Against expectations, they got along excellently with budgerigars, cardinals, and weaver birds from their African homeland. *Agapornis pullaria*, however, is of a very nervous temperament, and new imports are even dreadfully timid, which frequently leads to losses from delirious frenzies and subsequent injuries, including skull and other fractures.

This perhaps smallest of the lovebirds, measuring only 13.5 to 14.5 cm (5.3 to 5.7 inches) total body length, stands out because of its unusually brilliant plumage. Its reddish-green coloration is quite similar to that of the wings, and the underwing coverts in the female are mainly green. And there you have the most obvious distinguishing characteristics to tell the sexes apart. The frontal spot in the female is smaller, and more likely to be orange instead of blood red as in the male, and corresponds more closely to the German name "orange head" for these lovebirds. Blue feathers or plumage on the female's rump are scantier.

I've repeatedly read in the older literature that sexual differentiation of the Red-faced Lovebirds is supposed to be simple. Despite that, however, I hesitate agreeing, because I've often been in doubt about it myself. Moreover, I found many proven experts who agree with me on this point, and believe that sexing could be significantly more certain if based upon differences between male and female behavior. But that, too, seems so simple yet not so simple, though practice definitely does make the master, as the saying goes.

Likewise, I've read several times about allegedly pronounced brilliant blue on the upper part of the male's rump, yet I'm unable to remember ever having clearly observed it. Paintings can easily give a false impression. In the first place, not even the green parts of the plumage are uniformly colored in individual instances, and, in the second place, the bird's plumage is very rarely as immaculately glossy, smooth, and sleek as the painter would have it.

Any Red-faced Lovebirds on the market are certainly purebred, since nothing has been heard yet about any successful crosses. Moreover, breeding them is too difficult for the taste of most lovebird fanciers, who can have it so much easier with the other members of the genus. Even Hampe had serious problems with it back in the 1930s (The Nesting Habits of *Agapornis*

The Red-faced Lovebird has a distinct red patch of feathers on its tail.

Photo by Wolfgang de Grahl

pullaria, London 1937). Other top-of-the-line experts have often similarly tried (in vain) since then to breed Red-faced Lovebirds. The main difficulty is that birds of this species will not accept the hollows in tree stumps or rotted branches which we prepare for them, but insist on setting up the nesting sites themselves. And in doing so, the female distinguishes herself by performing most of the work, but has the male constantly watching her from nearby. This apparently involves a triggering stimulus which could be of considerable importance in achieving a successful brood. Under such conditions, the amateur breeder has little luck insisting on square wooden nesting boxes of any type, and not even a natural, hollowed-out tree stump makes any impression on the breeding pair.

In their central African homeland on the equator, the Red-faced Lovebirds gnaw and dig out nesting hollows in termite mounds. When the mounds are cut open, you can see how the long entrance tunnel runs first downward and then turns upward. The passage finally makes a right angle turn into the actual, pitch-black brooding hollow. The interior is loosely and thinly padded with various grasses, fragments of bark and dry grassheads, which the female tucked under her plumage and brought home. The otherwise valiant termites, strangely enough, don't attack these birds which are poking holes in their homes. Cooperation with the insects is more like it, and is of critical importance for the

structural stability of the gnawed-out passageways, which, during the insects' wanderings through them, are somehow cemented hard as rock with their bodily secretions. So an imported, but vacant termite hill would unfortunately not be any guarantee of success in breeding Red-faced Lovebirds, as appropriate as it may seem

Photo by Glenn Scott Axelrod

If you live where the weather permits, an outdoor aviary with lots of nest boxes, can produce bumper crops of young Red-faced Lovebirds and add some money to your available cash!

(South African hobbyists have had discouraging experience with it).

In England, encouraging results were obtained with a large ball of peat for use in building a nesting hollow. On the other hand, since bone-dry peat picks up the least amount of moisture, the embryos could possibly become fatalities.

Every nesting site in a European aviary (that is, in other than natural conditions in their homeland) would be best located in a shady corner so that the inside of the nesting hollow remains dark. The birds instinctively work in the dark and likewise brood and feed their young in complete darkness. No shaft of any light penetrates down into a termite hill, at the end of almost five feet of winding tunnel. Past-master Hampe himself set up an experimental heap of clay, sand, and slaked lime at least a yard high, but nothing very much ever came of it. Later, he was more successful with a wall made of soft clay or loam cubes through which an actual tunnel was gnawed, and at whose end was a grapefruit-sized hollow space. He even got the hen to lay her eggs in it. Yet although this level of success can often be reached, it's really not completely a success as long as embryos die in the eggshell. Who can finally explain the real causes for this?

Wooden crates provided with holes which are stuffed with ordinary garden peat are probably the best nesting boxes for hobbyists to use in their breeding efforts. The peat has to be thoroughly moistened first, and then pressed into the holes while still wet. Only in that way will the peat harden as it dries, thus holding solidly enough so it doesn't crumble and collapse later, and bury nest and hen alike under it.

The reader may find it useful to review some of the information from breeding reports which appeared over the last 50 years, and which are summarized as follows:

1. Red-faced Lovebirds are best introduced as groups of pairs into a spacious flight enclosure, where they can find material to build their own nesting hollow.

2. The clutch is usually between four and seven eggs.

3. The brood time is reported from Uganda as three and a half weeks. The new birds are nestlings for six weeks, according to Uganda sources. (None of the available sources of information are very reliable, and considerable contradictions pop up everywhere.)

4. Both parents feed the young.

5. The nestlings' thin downy feathers with their baby-pink shimmer are replaced in about 17 days by the first budding feather quills.

6. After a relatively long nestling time, the young Red-faced Lovebirds were a good seven weeks old when they took their first flight out of their dark birthplace.

7. A rather high temperature in the breeding hollow seems naturally to promote successful breeding. My research indicated that the inside temperature of a termite hill is 82.4° to 87.8°F. It's interesting that under such circumstances, humidity can never be as prevalent and important as specialists like so well to maintain.

8. In the wild, young Red-faced Lovebirds molt their adolescent plumage towards the end of their fourth month of life, and then become less and less distinguishable from the adult birds. In captivity, it seems the situation is essentially different, depending upon birthdate.

These lovebirds have been known since 1603. They were regularly kept as cage birds since the mid 18th century, according to reliable sources. Reports on their care and feeding, though, have been deplorably scant at all times.

Photo courtesy of Vogelpark Walsrode

Red-faced Lovebirds about one month old.

Although these little Africans don't like to eat from the ground, and in the wild even avoid staying down there too long, you should spread the feed for newly imported ones on the floor of the enclosure. *Agapornis pullaria* is distinctly an eater of grass seeds, and, during its first months after capture and export, hardly takes anything except light small-grained millet and seedheads. Bouquets of wild grasses are excellent supplemental foods, perhaps with lettuce seed, grass seed, and weed seed, depending upon the season.

My admittedly modest experience in these special cases has always indicated that specific birds react in highly individualized ways as far as seed preference goes. Some gourmets even accept mealworms, ant pupae and insects. Green figs could be a usable supplement, thick-barked branches are very acceptable for gnawing, and, luckily, most Red-faced Lovebirds like apples . . . and they like them best, according to my own tests, when the apple is cut into french-fry style strips and attached with clothespins to the cage wire for easy access to a beak.

Red-faced Lovebirds are in many respects just the right creatures for parrot fanciers who want to experiment. I'd like to remind you, by the way, that newly imported Red-faced Lovebirds are extremely susceptible to colds and so have to be kept very warm for the first month; you've got to provide for at least 77°F. Because of the initially enormous timidity and nervousness, try to go easy on them as much as possible. You never know just how the transfer to a garden enclosure will affect them; it's usually not so good during the same year they're imported. You can readily understand why their sale by mail order, pet shop or importer has become rather rare today. The question is whether it's reasonable to import more of them as long as there is so little probability of developing production of progeny to any stable level. Mortality is, as much as ever, greater than the average for all lovebirds, so should we decimate wild stocks? Those people who want to use that as an argument should be

A newly imported flock of Red-faced Lovebirds. Keeping many birds together is always a risk since they can fight and spread disease very easily. Only experts in the bird business should attempt this labor-savings.

immediately reassured, because the Red-faced Lovebird has the least to fear of all the lovebirds. Extinction may not even be possible! And that's a fine thought for the friends of these charming little parrots.

Not many Red-faced Lovebirds are seen at public bird shows, and anyone who knows the situation will certainly understand the reluctance of owners to show them. A lot of hustle and bustle is exactly what these dwarfs tolerate so poorly. Many long-time fanciers of the species even suggest that it's better to clip them to inhibit

their flight, at least when they're kept in cages, although that isn't always good for their appearance, and reduces their chances of winning prizes.

As already indicated, I've also occasionally sold Red-faced Lovebirds. Only with hesitation did I accept new ones. There was no lack of demand. Quite the opposite. But when you officially have birds for sale, you unfortunately can't make distinctions, such as which customer you want to have which parrot. Some of my Red-faced Lovebirds finally went to older people who, at

best, once cared for a budgerigar or a roller canary. For beginners like that, I wouldn't recommend this little lovebird. Many such attempts end unhappily.

But there's no rule without its exception! A little old lady who lived alone in a furnished room, despite all of my objections, would not be talked out of having a particularly disheveled and, in my opinion, sad-looking male. And she wanted just him alone. She had in mind for him to keep company with her old, green budgerigar female, which would "most assuredly become happier." The old lady stood in front of my showcase cage every day until I finally gave in and gave her the bird at a reduced price. Obviously, I was convinced that the stronger lovebird would sooner or later do the old budgerigar hen in, or would himself perish due to natural causes and loneliness. I didn't see my old customer for a long while, but I knew she was buying bird feed at the supermarket, which was conveniently located opposite her room.

It was winter again, and almost a year since I had sold the Red-faced Lovebird to the old woman, when a child came in, handed me a note and put some money down on the counter. The note asked me would I please come over to Mrs.____to trim her little parrot's nails. A little later I could hardly believe my eyes as I saw the aforementioned Red-faced Lovebird sitting on his owner's shoulder, where he gave twittering replies when spoken to, and enthusiastically flicked his nicely re-established, once-battered tail. There was no trace of the otherwise troublesome shyness so often seen in this species of lovebird. What an experience!

The British breeder Arthur A. Prestwich is supposed to be the only one to have succeeded in colonial breeding of Red-faceded Lovebirds in large aviaries for three years in a row. The information I received was that several dozen young birds were reared, which sounds unbelievable, but was apparently described in detail and confirmed. As far as American breeding successes are concerned, I couldn't discover anything significant, for example, from California, which otherwise is famous for such things.

The Red-faced Lovebird, *Agapornis pullaria*, **photographed in the San Diego Zoo.**

Photo by A.J.Mobbs

The Red-faced Lovebird, *Agapornis pullaria*. This is one of the birds from the breeding colony of Arthur A. Prestwich, the first person to colony breed this subspecies.

GREY-HEADED LOVEBIRD

AGAPORNIS CANA

The island nation of Madagascar (independent since 1960 as the Malagasy Republic) in the Indian Ocean off the east coast of Africa, is said to have banned exports of the Grey-headed or Madagascar Lovebird. On its 230,000 square miles of territory are high plateaus to about 4000 feet above sea level, and that's home for two slightly different races or varieties of the only Grey-headed Lovebirds native there. They have been introduced to the Comoros, Seychelles, Reunion, Rodriguez, Zanzibar and Mauritius, although hardly anything has been reported on those populations during the past several years. In 1979 I provided sport-diver friends of mine with identification photographs and paintings and asked them to be on the lookout for Grey-headed Lovebirds during their four weeks of vacation on the Seychelles. They didn't spot a single specimen, although they followed along many island coastlines in a rubber pneumatic boat. After the ban on exports from Madagascar, hobbyists might have been able to hope at least for birds born in captivity, but these prospects do not seem too good, either. Our import outlook here in Germany seems poor, and what breeders do accomplish is hardly encouraging.

Hampe had to report in his pioneering book on lovebirds that breeding does not always proceed smoothly, or even succeed regularly. What he circumvents so gracefully here in writing is, in a nutshell, that Grey-headed Lovebirds indeed often go willingly to brood, but despite perhaps even successful hatching, the young almost never reach the fledgling stage. The reasons are not at all clear. H. Lauer

Photo by Reinhard Tierfoto

The Grey-headed Lovebird from Madagascar (Malagasy). The male has the grey head.

wrote similarly on the many unpleasant incidents which can befall hobbyists who try breeding Grey-headed Lovebirds. On the other hand, old Neunzig spoke of productive broods.

The timid Madagascar Grey-heads are hardly ideal as cage birds. Few become tame or at least somewhat trusting, and their deficient vocal talent disappoints those who are hoping for it.

I understand that Grey-heads, like everything rare and expensive, are in demand by many bird fanciers. Yet, after all, they are not so enchantingly beautiful, as are, for me at least, Peach-faced Lovebirds.

The body length of these little lovebirds is only 13 to 14 cm (5 to 5.5 inches), and they seem more slender than their mainland African relatives, weighing only about an ounce (27 to 32 grams). The beak is conspicuously delicate in both sexes. The male's head, cheeks, throat and neck down to the shoulders are grayish white. The wings are brilliantly deep green, with distinctly lighter grass green underneath. Breast plumage can shimmer yellowish, and even a light violet undercolor (employees of a Dutch firm confirmed my observation, but had no explanation for the violet).

The females are easy to recognize, because the upper parts (which are grayish in males) are golden yellow/green. The upper part of the body seems lighter, while the dusky or black feathers are completely absent.

The sexes of Grey-headed Lovebirds born in captivity can be differentiated early, because the gray on the male's head shimmers through while he's still young.

The discovery of the only lovebird native to an area outside Africa goes back to the year 1788. And by the end of the last century, massive imports were entering Europe,

Photo courtesy of the San Diego Zoo

A magnificent, mature male *Agapornis cana*, the Grey-headed Lovebird from Madagascar.

thousands coming through Hamburg on ships travelling African routes. In a contemporary report from that time, I read that with the Grey-headed Lovebird the sexes were able to be separated quite well, which was thought to be necessary since the males were more attractive and much more good-natured. The dull and homely females on the other

Photo by Horst Mueller

Some male Grey-headed Lovebirds have an almost purple sheen to their feathers. It has no ring around the eye and has the shortest beak of all lovebirds.

hand, were muderous she-devils who overpowered and mercilessly hacked to pieces all equally sized or even larger fellow lodgers in enclosures or cages.

An old acquaintance of mine who bred lovebirds gave up on the otherwise successful colonial breeding of his Grey-head lines, and housed his six pairs in separate compartments. Despite ample space replete with places to hide, older birds regularly pursued and attacked the young of the other pairs. If several broods were simultaneously at the

fledgling stage, and one of the young begged food from the wrong adult, he got no food but beak slashes from the female, causing heavily bleeding wounds. In one case, two hopefully begging youngsters were even killed.

These Madagascar Lovebirds are best allowed ample freedom of movement. If you want to believe the majority of published experiences, they're frostproof, winterproof, insensitive to European autumn and winter weathers, and are supposed to be able to winter in open-air enclosures, even without any heating. On the other hand, the bird fanciers I asked unanimously reported that the Grey-headed Lovebird certainly does not like a great deal of air movement, and for that reason is sensitive to drafts.

I can well imagine that people who claim such climatic hardiness for the Grey-heads have perhaps personally never kept them in garden enclosures during the winter. Since my own experience in this matter was not complete, I did some research for the sake of my readers. As a result, I ask my readers not to refer to me, or blame me, if they insist in testing the alleged robust constitution of their Grey-headed Lovebirds in winter and frost.

Like any other passionate bird fancier, I am also very interested in so-called rarities, although rarity would not necessarily be any reason for purchasing one. Instead, I often look for birds in zoos and on bird farms, or visit private hobbyists and listen to their experiences. In that

context I'll pass on Dutch and Belgian experiences that Grey-headed Lovebirds are susceptible to clinging humidity, long periods of continuous rain, dips in temperature along with stormy winds and even light night frosts. I observed in both of these neighboring countries that the outdoor flights of breeding aviaries were protected from wind with wire-reinforced glass.

In one of my sales aviaries some Grey-headed Lovebirds died despite being under cover, because they perched next to an outside wall which cooled way down on winter nights. Practical experience obviously contradicts statements in the scant early literature. So, I share the breeder's opinion that Grey-headed Lovebirds either need a thoroughly heated overnight refuge as soon as temperatures drop below 50°F, or else they must be brought into the house.

An old lovebird specialist in Antwerp, Belgium, advised me to separate the sexes while they were in the wintering enclosure, so they couldn't see or hear one another. Only in that way could bloody fights be prevented, the old expert assured me, because at times other than the breeding season even firmly committed mates got very rough with one another.

Can several pairs really be kept together all year in one aviary, as one occasionally reads? To answer that, I can only contribute the information that in collective enclosures, no really dangerous biting occurs, but neither does any pairing up of mates or preparations for any reproduction, either. A word to the specialist dealer needs to be emphasized: newly imported Grey-headed Lovebirds are definitely not a risk-free addition to your stock of saleable birds! Better start with the *personata* group of lovebirds (Black-masked, Black-cheeked, Fischer's, Nyasa).

Perhaps the poor outlook for breeding is still the reason for the Grey-head's lack of popularity even among specialized lovebird enthusiasts. Once you get to know importers, you will find that Grey-headed Lovebirds arrive in far worse condition than the other, lovebirds; their losses are greater, too, during quarantine and in the holding enclosure as well. Despite my good contacts, however, they were tight-lipped as to their source of the birds, most of which were shipped further on to California. German importers have little to say about Grey-headed Lovebirds, or else have forgotten what they once knew because this species often remained out of sight for decades at a time. In the U.S.A., on the other hand, you can't rightly speak of scant supplies of Grey-headed Lovebirds.

In the light of international pronouncements on the subject of breeding, the main difficulty evidently resides in the fact that the preferred breeding season occurs during our cold November to December period, and apparently any change in this instinctive behavior or biological rhythm is hardly possible, even with the greatest patience. Even birds reared here show breeding fervor often enough in the winter, and you can well imagine what problems that causes. As far as breeding is concerned, every country with a warm climate has a great advantage from the very start.

Besides its use during the breeding season, the nesting box also serves for sleeping and temporary refuge in bad weather, as their African relatives know it. A community arrangement in

Eric Peake drew what he called a pair of Grey-headed Lovebirds based upon dead specimens of the first import. The head of the female looks suspicious.

large exhibition aviaries is possible, I believe, with other birds of at least equal or larger size. But I'd like to recommend introducing only the Grey-headed male, who is prettier anyway, as the sole representative of the lovebirds. His voice has always reminded me of the Peach-face; the noise level remains within tolerable limits, however, in proportion to the smaller size, which is a blessing, for the Grey-head has the habit of persistently participating.

Those who keep these birds should know that they, like sparrows, forage around on the ground significantly more often than other lovebirds.

German-bred birds, according to the experience of the relatively few breeders here, are hardier in tolerating typical European bad-weather summers, less timid towards strangers, and don't bite nearly as much as birds captured in the wild. Be careful about that biting, though, for if you grab hold of them, they twist around and use their delicate, harmless-looking beak to hack painful, difficult-to-heal holes in your thumb. Wear gloves!

Although the former French colonials of Madagascar were among the traditional and enthusiastic lovers of the bird world, there are only sparse reports on the life of the Grey-headed Lovebirds in the wild. Their preference for hollow tree trunks or branches for brooding has been reported, as well as how the male likes to sit in this nest, in which, somewhat at a lower level, the female tends to her clutch of eggs.

An acceptable solution in the enclosure appears to be the use of ordinarily available cockatiel nesting boxes. The chances of success are considerably improved if the breeder provides three boxes from which the birds can select their own. I'll let my deceased colleague Carl Aschenborn describe the further course of the event:

"The nest is constructed of bark and leaf fragments, preferably willow, which the female tucks under her back or rump feathers and carries into the box.

The clutch usually consists of four eggs, which are ready in about 21 days. The young leave the nest box when they're about five weeks old. When they become independent they should be separated from their parents as a preventive measure, particularly when the parents start working towards another brood."

The first large feathers, which push up through the skin, show up surprisingly early, sometimes as soon as the ninth or tenth day.

It was obvious to me that in stories about the behavior of Grey-headed Lovebirds, highly individual habits popped up, like hens whose instinct to chew up nest-padding materials into small pieces and take them into the nest is only weakly developed or non-existent, who lose most of the materials just after tucking them under their feathers, and then pay no further attention to it. On the other hand, I still hear the lament of a breeder of Grey-headed Lovebirds whose best breeding hen never wanted to stop all the carrying and nest building, even after all her eggs had been laid. She buried eggs which she had already begun to incubate, and in which the embryos died of undercooling or of oxygen deprivation. He got it down to a science to identify the proper moment for removing all building materials. Stories about the many incidents which threaten the breeder's success are absolutely believable.

During this period, the male is an attentive, devoted spouse who not uncommonly wants

to provide food so assiduously that his mate cannot handle the amount at all. Tirelessly he keeps her company at and in the nesting box, and also sometimes chases away curious mischief-makers.

As concerns feeding, the collection of wild weed seeds is recommendable, such as couchgrass, chickweed, ribwort, etc. Those are good supplements for rearing feeds, though fresh millet heads certainly also do a good job. I've read that the stomach contents of Grey-headed

Photo courtesy of Vogelpark Walsrode

A male Grey-headed Lovebird.

Lovebirds shot during the brooding period show that they rear their young chiefly on insects, worms, and beetles. A zoo keeper pointed out to me that although seeds would be very fondly eaten, the seeds have to be cracked a bit first to avoid too much wastage. Left to their own devices, the birds would have difficulty cracking the hard husks. Just as a precaution, I'm passing this information on.

I've tried to bring together information on a little parrot that was once very familiar in Germany as an ornamental

cage and aviary bird, but one which bird fanciers almost let become extinct in favor of the more colorful members, which are now the most favorite ornamental birds of parrot fanciers. It's hardly believable that even shortly after WWI the Madagascar Lovebird, as the Grey-headed Lovebird was called, was one of the three popular lovebirds in Europe's bird collections. Should we even be considering here in this practical book a small parrot which is only rarely found on the market? To answer that, the importation of Grey-headed Lovebirds can indeed be improved once again, for, after all, these birds are numerous in their huge native territory, and not yet endangered.

In America the situation is quite different because Grey-headed Lovebirds are very much in demand and can be bought in any of the better pet shops, certainly in every large city on the West coast, as I've seen. Sufficient numbers of Grey-headed Lovebirds are bred and available in California. It was here in 1948–1953 that imported Madagascan Grey-heads were most numerous and popular, while German hobbyists were beginning again at zero. It's no wonder that American breeding of Grey-headed Lovebirds ran so successfully, with such plentiful starting materials.

In the wild, Grey-headed Lovebirds are apparently brush birds which, when startled, are more likely to hop from branch to branch than to fly far away. That makes capture of escaped birds more likely, since escapees remain nearby within calling distances of their group. It would also be possible to let a bird of a firmly mated pair fly free for an hour.

Just for completeness, I have to mention that the so-called Rodriguez Grey-headed Lovebird (*Agapornis cana ablectanea*) *wa*s the species which was imported in great numbers into western Europe at the turn of the century; *Agapornis cana* is, however, still the main form.

From England, I learned that young Grey-heads were successfully and repeatedly reared by "nursemaid" budgerigar hens. And that's an interesting tip for many readers. It's something which would certainly be favored by the small size of the Grey-headed Lovebird, though I doubt that this trick works too often.

While I mentioned that startled Grey-heads don't take off and cover any great distances, that shouldn't imply that they're only moderately good flyers. Quite the contrary. It was by flying that they could have once reached Madagascar from the African mainland. Why they don't try to go back, no one knows. No reintroductions into Africa were attempted, which is hardly surprising since there are enough complaints about their damage to crops on their native island. You've probably already thought that there are no color varieties (mutations) of *Agapornis cana*, yet I'm thoroughly convinced that they could be produced just as they have been with others of the genus. The obstacle was and remains that hobbyists in Germany have too few of them. A gray head

along with a pure white, yellow, or other colored body should be attractive, but I'm not prepared to go into the genetics of just what color varieties we could create successfully.

In the literature I've received nothing is stated about crosses with other

members to the genus *Agapornis*, though I consider a cross with *Agapornis pullaria* (Red-faced Lovebird) the most likely. I don't think it's possible to cross a Grey-headed Lovebird with a budgerigar, although one was reported almost a hundred years ago in Germany.

A female Grey-headed Lovebird, *Agapornis cana* from Madagascar.

Photo courtesy of the San Diego Zoo

ADVICE AND SUGGESTIONS

Readers often need information urgently, so, mindful of my own helplessness in the beginning, I'd like to answer a few questions here, such as: What can you do when the parents don't feed their young as they're supposed to do? What can you do when they pluck out a young bird's pretty new feathers? How do you buy birds without being "taken"? How do you get color varieties?

FEEDING BABIES

If a hobbyist suddenly has to feed young lovebirds himself for whatever reason, he soon realizes that the process is much simpler with finches, who open their bills wide. Parrots, on the other hand, take the beak of their youngster sideways, forming somewhat of a close connection through which to pass the regurgitated pap. That's why the natives feed the young parrots they take from the nest by giving them chewed cud from their own mouth, a method Europeans don't take to comfortably. We prefer spoons or food injectors, but then have to keep the container of pap at body temperature (about 98.6°F) in a water bath (or in a double boiler). The little food recipients, too, should be comfortably warm, because if they're cold, they hardly open their beaks.

I don't think much of suggestions which involve a uniform number of hand-feedings every 24 hours at specified intervals. Haven't

such recommendations caused enough misery for infants? Even the beginner can recognize just how much the bird's crop is holding, whether in a new nestling or in an older youngster whose plumage is starting to appear. I didn't know any better way to do it when I started. Feeding pauses shouldn't last until the crop empties; otherwise the digestion time cannot and will not be uniform. As long as the crop is still visibly 25 to 30% full, you don't have to rush with your hand-feeding, even if you exceed the length of the intervals you may have seen somewhere. An exception to the rule which experts can break: if the young bird begs you for food, give just a taste so as to build the bird's confidence in you. Otherwise, I believe it's improbable that insessorial or nidiculous birds (i.e. birds which remain in the nest a while after hatching) of this age can gauge their own intake. Don't forget to clean off any messy beaks, at least for purposes of hygiene.

The progress of body growth is more reliably followed with a letter or household balance (or scales), not merely by eye. If growth continues smoothly, the pap doesn't have to be so thinly diluted. Beginners do well to adjust the consistency of the pap with clean water, not with milk, which sours easily. If possible, try to mix in some softened (swollen) seeds; with such small quantities, you can easily remove the husks from the larger seeds.

Finally, when the first large feathers begin growing, and a lot of energy is needed, more animal protein would be helpful; the simplest way to get it is in a soft feed mix available at the pet shop. Curds, too, are rich in it. Besides the egg food already mentioned, as well as the proven ready-mixed rearing foods, which can be enriched in various ways, here are two formulas based upon my own good experience:

1. Baby food, stirred and mixed in equal proportion with oatmeal flakes softened in warm water. Add a teaspoonful of either raw or soft-boiled egg yolk and sweeten with two "pinches" (two blobs that fit on a knife point) of honey.

2. In a thermos bottle mix cooled light millet which has been soaked in hot water for several hours until soft and swollen plus some boiled oatmeal or groat porridge. Add a teaspoonful of ant pupae or ready-mixed soft feed for frail insectivorous birds, and then mix in a finely chopped green lettuce leaf.

During the last stage of development, break up or grind a mixture of oats, wheat and the contents of large sunflower seeds, and give it to help the transition to self-feeding. Control any diarrhea by adding some poppy seed to the mix.

The rewards for all this time and effort is, as is well known, a charmingly tame and tremendously devoted bunch of birds. However, hand-reared parrots have to be kept apart, and you have to occupy yourself quite a bit with them. If you turn them back to their fellow birds, they lose some of their special trust and confidence in you, and that would be a shame.

WHEN THE YOUNG ARE PLUCKED

A mother's plucking out the feathers from her defenseless nestlings is, thank heavens, no longer a usual problem among lovebirds. This bad habit is most often seen in Fischer's Lovebirds. The parts of the body most at risk are the lower nape of the neck and upper back just between the wings.

Females who have never plucked before can suddenly begin, then stop it just as suddenly the following year. From my own experience, I've found that the plucking (violent enough to draw blood) of young birds in earlier decades was more common than now because of the much more primitive accommodations and the much less imaginative and less rational diets. Yet, there are cases reported among birds in the wild following war, defoliation and large-scale application of chemical agents, and also following extensive forest fires in Lower Saxony (an area encompassing Hanover, Oldeburg, Braunschweig, etc. in Germany) and Canada. That implies external influences and the resulting signs of deficiency. Understandably, vitamin D deficiency was long included among the probable causes of plucking. Reliable information on the triggering factors is still lacking, thus making

prevention a matter of luck. Parasitic infestation, such as with mites, ticks or lice, is certainly not the cause of the abnormal behavior of plucking the feathers out of their youngsters.

In general, the violently plucked feathers regrow quickly and without any problems. Every experienced breeder has, of course, had fatalities from blood loss and undercooling among still very young nestlings, but, on the whole, very little residual damage to most birds in their care. One risky situation I experienced, however, was that the young were plucked just before their first fledgling flight, and had to remain in the nesting box. The impatient female, again seized with breeding ardor, threw the poor creatures out, and they fell to their death.

You can carefully remove gnawed-off, bent or broken feather stumps from healthy nestlings. You can remove blood stains, if you want to, simply with a cotton swab dipped into warm water. Sulforamide powder accelerates wound healing. I do not advise salve or ointment, or iodine, which is too strong. Some commercially available products may be useful in reducing feather plucking in some cases. I do not advocate the use of cod liver oil.

This distressing surprise almost always occurs at a time when the brood still needs parental feeding. If you decide against hand-feeding, then a solution is possible that permits all the beak contact they need, but only that; the parents can feed their young, but are obstructed from

plucking out their plumage. Devices to achieve this include mini-cages hung next to the nesting box, at about half the height of the box, and wire mesh dividers. These devices are also suitable for protecting the young from persecution by their own parents who are about to go into another period of breeding fervor.

For 11 years I tried to run down and get to the root of all the recommendations that are rather regularly praised as successfull methods to stop plucking. It turned out that actual, isolated successes were praised too hastily and could not be repeated simply by following the recommendations, which was disappointing to say the least.

The process of healing the skin wounds—mainly regrowth of plucked out feathers—vastly increases the young birds' need for protein. They should receive high-potency dietary protein to supply the necessary building blocks, the amino acids, especially arginine and glycine.

Let me quickly dispel the widely spread erroneous idea that young parrots plucked by their parents will later do the same thing to themselves and become so-called feather eaters. Moreover, there's no reason to believe that plucking is an inherited defect.

DIVERGENT PLUMAGE COLORS (MUTATIONS)

Most changes that occur by themselves (mutations) are based upon a hereditary defect, which negatively affects the survival capability of the abnormal bird. Often enough these "random products" perish before they have a chance to transmit their randomly changed hereditary burden to any offspring, or else they are infertile from the very start and couldn't transmit it anyway. Any offspring produced, however, become carriers of the random mutations in their genetic constitution, because it's recognized that it stabilizes, so to speak, and doesn't return to normal on its own. Unusual-looking birds would have only little chance of survival in the wild. The breeder, however, protects and nurtures them with all the means at his disposal to have them reproduce. That's, so to speak, the crux of the matter when breeding for mutations in ornamental birds.

You can hardly evaluate the genetic make-up of birds just from their outward appearance, if they are heterozygous for various traits. Which of these will later come to light after they mate will depend to a large extent upon the genetic make-up of their mates. It will also depend upon what succeeds in "getting through," that is, what is dominant. What is suppressed or masked by the stronger, dominant character is not apparent (although it is transmitted) in the offspring, and is logically called *recessive*. Only two *homozygous* (pure for certain trait) birds always produce the same kind of offspring. Take a look in the encyclopedia under heredity and Mendelian laws for details about all of this. Predicted results, however, refer only to each one hundred offspring (i.e., a probability percentage), and

do not necessarily apply to individual broods. There is quite a bit of specialized literature on the genetics of bird breeding, so there's no need for too much here.

Decades of painstaking research on the well-known budgerigar revealed the theory and principles by which definite color varieties could be bred. Those complex tables, feared by many bird fanciers, depicting combinations of chromosomes, etc., won't be reproduced here, since there's no room, anyway. But their absence doesn't detract from this book, for informative articles on the subject appear regularly in the ornithological and hobbyist literature. Happily, basic studies are not needed for every parrot species. The road to reach our objective as lovebird color breeders is the same road taken by budgerigar fanciers. The only important reservation, however, in that the budgerigar doesn't have very close relatives; the lovebirds, at least in breeding enclosures, engage in mixed matings, so the color breeding principles from the budgerigar literature are applicable only if the lovebirds are purebred, that is, not bastardized, which you often cannot find out or see.

SELECTION OF NEW BIRDS

If we look for a source of lovebirds, there are several possibilities. Importing your own from Africa, which I was occasionally able to do, is almost out of the question today for the individual as a private citizen. Collectors in Africa are not very interested in small shipments. The customer would have to pay

shipping materials, preliminary local transportation, air freight, customs and taxes, all probably amounting to much too high a cost. And if that weren't enough, he'd also have to come up with the expenses and risks of legally required quarantine! Mortality caused by transportation or medications make the whole deal unprofitable. A few wholesale importers may also sell retail now and then to an individual, but prefer their normal business with brokers, wholesalers, and established retailers.

Pet shops and breeders sell lovebirds. Domestically bred lovebirds, preferable for beginners, are not as common on the market, nor are various color varieties, which are best obtained from breeders. Hobbyist and breeder magazines run numerous ads for both sellers and buyers.

Then there are various bird centers, farms, zoos, and mail order firms. It's a matter of personal feeling whether you want to buy birds unseen, prepaid or postpaid, at your own risk during transportation, based upon the promises made in a newspaper advertisement. That's not for me. Unless fellow hobbyists or club members recommend a source, I consider it more advisable to make an appointment and personally visit the seller. Then you can see right away how the merchandise has been living. If you want to take a look at living animals before buying them, then give yourself sufficient time to observe enough. Experts warn us urgently not to be pushed to make instant decisions just because, for example, the seller all of a sudden says he has a lot of work to do and little time to waste.

OBSERVING PROSPECTIVE BIRDS

Sick birds hold themselves conspicuously stiller than their healthy fellow birds. No vigorous bird "sleeps" for long in broad daylight. It's better to forego buying birds, especially parrots, which sit, all fluffed up, on both feet, and which tuck their head or at least their beak into their feathers once everything has quieted down again.

Very skinny birds, too, should be left right where they are. The ridge of the breastbone should not stick out enough to be very visible; that would indicate malnutrition. Matted or soiled feathers around the vent indicate digestive disorders.

Experts consider the eyes as excellent indicators of health; they shouldn't look dull or sunken in. When the bird squints at frequent intervals, it's better to forego that bird.

The condition of the plumage is immediately apparent to the beginner, but, unless it's extremely bad and implies plucking, it's not too important. More activity and a chance to bathe usually bring rapid improvement. And the best food helps too.

Important note: When selecting, always stand somewhat back from the enclosure and wait. As long as the tenants fly excitedly around, you will hardly be able to see very much of the indicators of health, which

you want to spot. Startled or excited birds, even when quite afflicted, act lively and normal. What you really want to see is how they behave once they're calmed down again. That's crucial.

If you're a real animal lover, you've not only completely set up the accommodations but also filled the feed and water containers before you left to purchase your lovebirds. You have also realized that rapid change of environment, cage or enclosure, and not uncommonly also the feed, is stressful. Frequent monitoring of the new arrivals at first is always advisable.

LEGAL FORMALITIES FOR NEW BREEDERS

If you've never tried to breed parakeets or parrots, you should be aware that in certain areas private breeding is subject to regulation. Moreover, all these birds bred in captivity must be banded. Your local bird club or pet shop will advise you of local conditions and regulations.

If you keep individual pairs of lovebirds for their company and don't let them breed, then you'll only come into contact with the authorities in the rather unlikely event of ornithosis (previously called psitticosis, or parrot fever).

These two *Agapornis personata personnata* adorned the cover of the German edition of this book.

Photo by Reinhard Tierfoto

It is much wiser to buy finger-tamed lovebirds from your local pet shop. Most people don't have the time to spend to tame and train their lovebirds.